Veloce *Classic Reprint* Series

🇬🇧 British 250cc Racing Motorcycles

1946 to 1959: an era of ingenious innovation

Tim Bolton

Also from Veloce Publishing -

Enthusiast's Restoration Manual Series
Beginner's Guide to Classic Motorcycle Restoration, The (Burns)
Classic Large Frame Vespa Scooters, How to Restore (Paxton)
Ducati Bevel Twins 1971 to 1986 (Falloon)
How to Restore Classic Off-road Motorcycles (Burns)
How to restore Honda CX500 & CX650 – YOUR step-by-step colour illustrated guide to complete restoration (Burns)
How to restore Honda Fours – YOUR step-by-step colour illustrated guide to complete restoration (Burns)
Triumph Trident T150/T160 & BSA Rocket III, How to Restore (Rooke)
Yamaha FS1-E, How to Restore (Watts)

Essential Buyer's Guide Series
BMW Boxer Twins (Henshaw)
BMW E30 3 Series 1981 to 1994 (Hosier)
BMW GS (Henshaw)
BSA 350, 441 & 500 Singles (Henshaw)
BSA 500 & 650 Twins (Henshaw)
BSA Bantam (Henshaw)
Choosing, Using & Maintaining Your Electric Bicycle (Henshaw)
Ducati Bevel Twins (Falloon)
Ducati Desmodue Twins (Falloon)
Ducati Desmoquattro Twins – 851, 888, 916, 996, 998, ST4 1988 to 2004 (Falloon)
Hinckley Triumph triples & fours 750, 900, 955, 1000, 1050, 1200 – 1991-2009 (Henshaw)
Honda CBR FireBlade (Henshaw)
Honda CBR600 Hurricane (Henshaw)
Honda SOHC Fours 1969-1984 (Henshaw)
Kawasaki Z1 & Z900 (Orritt)
Moto Guzzi 2-valve big twins (Falloon)
Norton Commando (Henshaw)
Royal Enfield Bullet (Henshaw)
Triumph 350 & 500 Twins (Henshaw)
Triumph Bonneville (Henshaw)
Triumph Thunderbird, Trophy & Tiger (Henshaw)
Velocette 350 & 500 Singles 1946 to 1970 (Henshaw)
Vespa Scooters – Classic 2-stroke models 1960-2008 (Paxton)

Biographies
Chris Carter at Large – Stories from a lifetime in motorcycle racing (Carter & Skelton)
Edward Turner – The Man Behind the Motorcycles (Clew)
Jim Redman – 6 Times World Motorcycle Champion: The Autobiography (Redman)
Mike The Bike – Again (Macauley)
'Sox' – Gary Hocking – the forgotten World Motorcycle Champion (Hughes)

General
BMW Boxer Twins 1970-1995 Bible, The (Falloon)
BMW Cafe Racers (Cloesen)

BMW Custom Motorcycles – Choppers, Cruisers, Bobbers, Trikes & Quads (Cloesen)
British 250cc Racing Motorcycles (Pereira)
British Café Racers (Cloesen)
British Custom Motorcycles – The Brit Chop – choppers, cruisers, bobbers & trikes (Cloesen)
BSA Bantam Bible, The (Henshaw)
BSA Motorcycles – the final evolution (Jones)
Ducati 750 Bible, The (Falloon)
Ducati 750 SS 'round-case' 1974, The Book of the (Falloon)
Ducati 860, 900 and Mille Bible, The (Falloon)
Ducati Monster Bible (New Updated & Revised Edition), The (Falloon)
Ducati Story, The - 6th Edition (Falloon)
Ducati 916 (updated edition) (Falloon)
Funky Mopeds (Skelton)
How your motorcycle works (Henshaw)
Italian Cafe Racers (Cloesen)
Italian Custom Motorcycles (Cloesen)
Japanese Custom Motorcycles – The Nippon Chop – Chopper, Cruiser, Bobber, Trikes and Quads (Cloesen)
Kawasaki Triples Bible, The (Walker)
Kawasaki Z1 Story, The (Sheehan)
Moto Guzzi Sport & Le Mans Bible, The (Falloon)
The Moto Guzzi Story - 3rd Edition (Falloon)
Motorcycle Apprentice (Cakebread)
Motorcycle GP Racing in the 1960s (Pereira)
Motorcycle Road & Racing Chassis Designs (Noakes)
Motorcycling in the '50s (Clew)
MV Agusta Fours, The book of the classic (Falloon)
Norton Commando Bible – All models 1968 to 1978 (Henshaw)
Scooters & Microcars, The A-Z of Popular (Dan)
Scooter Lifestyle (Grainger)
Scooter Mania! – Recollections of the Isle of Man International Scooter Rally (Jackson)
Trikes, the little book of (Quellin)
Triumph Bonneville Bible (59-83) (Henshaw)
Triumph Bonneville!, Save the – The inside story of the Meriden Workers' Co-op (Rosamond)
Triumph Motorcycles & the Meriden Factory (Hancox)
Triumph Speed Twin & Thunderbird Bible (Woolridge)
Triumph Tiger Cub Bible (Estall)
Triumph Trophy Bible (Woolridge)
TT Talking – The TT's most exciting era – As seen by Manx Radio TT's lead commentator 2004-2012 (Lambert)
Velocette Motorcycles – MSS to Thruxton – Third Edition (Burris)
Vespa – The Story of a Cult Classic in Pictures (Uhlig)
Vincent Motorcycles: The Untold Story since 1946 (Guyony & Parker)

www.veloce.co.uk

First published under ISBN 978-1-904788-12-6 in 2004. Veloce Publishing Ltd., Veloce House, Parkway Farm Business Park, Middle Farm Way, Poundbury, Dorchester DT1 3AR, England. Tel 01305 260068. Fax 01305 268864. E-mail: veloce@veloce.co.uk. Web: www.veloce.co.uk
Veloce Classic Reprint edition published April 2018.
ISBN 978-1-787113-29-9/UPC 6-36847-01329-5

Readers with ideas for automotive books, or books on other transport or related hobby subjects, are invited to write to the editorial director of Veloce Publishing at the above address.
British Library Cataloguing in Publication Data -A catalogue record for this book is available from the British Library. Typesetting, design and page make-up all by Veloce on Apple Mac.
Printed and bound by CPI Group (UK) Ltd, Croydon, CR0 4YY.

Veloce *Classic Reprint* Series

British 250cc Racing Motorcycles

1946 to 1959: an era of ingenious innovation

Chris Pereira

VELOCE PUBLISHING
THE PUBLISHER OF FINE AUTOMOTIVE BOOKS

Contents

Acknowledgements
& Author's foreword

For their assistance with my research, and for allowing me access to their personal photographic collections, I would like to thank the following: Cecil Sandford, Bill Lomas, Dan Shorey, Gerry Turner, Jim Dakin, Teddy Kempson, Rob Foster, Harry Pearce, John Paterson, Les Leach, VMCC Librarian Annice Collett, VMCC Photographic Printer David Dalton, SR Keig Ltd., and Gordon Francis. I am also indebted to Rod Grainger of Veloce Publishing for taking on this project. Last, but by no means least, I would like to thank my wife Sondra, for her support and understanding during the time spent putting this book together.

Author's foreword

I offer no apologies for writing a book about a period in racing history which may already be forgotten. It is inconceivable that all the unique machines, together with the men who built and raced them, should completely disappear from history. While conducting my research, it was a great privilege to meet and talk with many former riders, all of whom expressed great interest in and enthusiasm for the project. However, had I been aware of the problems involved in trying to find a publisher, and the prohibitive cost of copyright fees, this book may not have been written. That it reached the publication stage is entirely due to my great respect and admiration for the riders and constructors who are featured in it. Lest they be forgotten for their part, however small, in creating motorcycle racing history; this book is dedicated to them.

Chris Pereira
Bracknell, England

Introduction

The 250cc class in Britain during the first decade after the second world war was, from a technical point of view, an extremely interesting and innovative period. This was entirely due to a lack of foresight on the part of British motorcycle manufacturers in failing to produce new 250cc racing machines. It was the desire to keep this class of racing alive that prompted so many talented individuals to build the many 'Specials' and hybrids that evolved during the decade. At first, many of the pre-war racing machines, such as Rudge, Excelsior and New Imperial, were restored and pressed into service. This led to the evolution of Specials based on extensively-modified, particularly with regard to suspension and brakes, pre-war machines. By the early 1950s, the use of Manx Norton and KTT Velocette engines, reduced to 250cc, also became popular, and a new line of hybrids evolved. A small minority of single-minded individuals went even further, and designed and built new engines, and even completely new machines.

Ironically, considering the number of gifted designers/engineers who were involved in private racing projects, the technical stagnation that existed in the British motorcycle industry is somewhat surprising. One can but wonder what might have been achieved had some of these designs received the benefit of industry backing and development.

The 250cc class in Britain in the 1950s was, therefore, to a great extent the preserve of the independent Special-builders. These enthusiasts produced machines which were to remain competitive for more than a decade, until genuine production racing machines arrived from the Continent. Although many of the British machines became less competitive against the foreign opposition, at National and Club racing level they still formed the bulk of the race entries throughout the 1950s, and a few remained in contention until well into the 1960s.

To mention every single 250cc Special built and raced between 1946 and 1959 would be an almost impossible task. It is, however, the intention here to provide information on the history and development of some of the more well-known machines, and on the men who built and rode them.

Chapter 1
The pre-war machines

Road racing in Britain got off to a slow start in 1946. As well as the shortage of new racing machines, fuel rationing was still in force, of course, and there was a serious dearth of road race circuits. The first major road race of 1946 was the Manx Grand Prix, followed a couple of weeks later by the first race meeting at Scarborough, on the newly-completed Oliver's Mount road circuit. Initially, the pre-war British machines had the 250cc class to themselves. By 1947, however, their biggest threat was the much-modified, pre-war Moto Guzzi ridden by Maurice Cann, who had begun to establish his dominance of the 250cc class.

Pike Rudge

At first, the most successful challenge to Maurice Cann's domination was provided by Roland Pike, an engineer from Edgware in Middlesex, on his modified, home-tuned Rudge. Roland and his brother Stan had raced Rudges before the war, and had ridden in the Manx Grand Prix and the TT. Preferring to use the two valve version on the grounds of simplicity and reliability, Roland steadily developed the very basic Rudge Rapid engine, ultimately achieving remarkable performance while still retaining exceptional reliability. Roland's engines also employed many special components (which he himself had developed), and later versions had bronze and then alloy cylinder heads. The Pike Rudge was further updated over the years, with particular modifications to brakes and suspension. Roland built his own frames, fitted with swinging arm rear suspension of his own design, in which the Newton-type hydraulic suspension units were angled steeply forwards. At first, he preferred to keep the relatively light girder forks, but eventually changed them for BSA telescopic forks with hydraulic damping. By 1950, the final version was an exceptionally neat

Rudge T.T.

1947 Stan Pike   68.56 5ᵗ
1948 Roland Pike 71.86 2nd
1949 Stan Pike   69.08 7ᵗʰ
1950 Roland Pike 74.14 4ᵗʰ
1951 Harold Hartley 67.92 10ᵗʰ
1952 Charlie Salt 75.06 10ᵗʰ
1953 Jackie Horne   15ᵗʰ
1954 Jackie Horne 75.64 10ᵗʰ
1949 Roland Pike   72.80 3rd

Rudge in Ulster GP

1949 Roland Pike 6ᵗʰ
1951 Bill Webster 8ᵗʰ

The ubiquitous pre-war, 250cc two-valve Rudge, which formed the basis for many post-war Specials. (Courtesy Beaulieu Archives)

2nd 71·86

Rudge guru Roland Pike with his 1948 TT machine. This has swinging arm rear suspension, but retains the original girder forks. (Courtesy SR Keig)

1st Maurice Cann Moto Guzzi 75 18

machine, with its characteristic long exhaust pipe terminating in a moderately large megaphone which extended well past the rear wheel spindle. The success of his machine led to the construction of many other Rudge-based Specials, also referred to as Pike Rudges, most of them incorporating special components supplied by Roland.

During 1946 and 1947, Roland recorded several wins and placings at Cadwell Park, and in 1948 he was second to Maurice Cann's Guzzi in the Lightweight TT, at 71.86mph (116.4km/h). He was third in 1949 when, once again, he was headed by two Guzzis. During practice, though, the Rudge had been timed at 93.77mph (151.90km/h), on the Sulby straight. In the 1950 TT, Roland finished in a worthy fourth place. The Pike Rudge was ridden in the TT for the last time in 1952, by which time Roland had joined BSA as a development engineer working on the Gold Star engine.

CTS

Another early example of a Rudge-based machine was the CTS. Built by Chris Tattersall and raced in the TT, both pre-war and post-war, the CTS was based on the Rudge Python four valve engine, though with lightened flywheels, and a Rudge four speed gearbox. A few examples of the CTS, using Hawill brakes and modified frames with plunger rear suspension, were built to order for other riders.

Horne Rudge

One of the neatest and most up-to-date versions of a 250 Rudge was built in 1953 by ex-racing man Greg Horne, from Perth in Scotland, for his son Jackie. The Horne Rudge was based on a 1936 Rudge Rapid engine and gearbox, mounted in a very modern, semi-duplex frame with twin top rails and a single front down tube which ran under the engine. The welded-on rear sub-frame carried the damper units for the swinging arm rear suspension, and the front forks were AMC telescopics. Initially, the two valve head was modified to use hairpin valve springs. The engine continued to be developed by the Hornes in their modestly-equipped home workshop. The cylinder head, for example, was replaced by a light alloy unit with bronze valve seats and hairpin valve springs. Ultimately, all that remained of the original engine were the crankcases and the crankshaft.

Jackie Horne rode the Rudge in the TT, finishing fifteenth in 1953 and tenth in 1954, and in the Ulster Grand Prix and the North West 200. His most successful year was 1955, when he won the 250cc Scottish Championships, and scored a string of wins at Errol, Crimmond and Kirkcaldy. TE (Tom) Rutherford acquired the Horne Rudge and raced it quite successfully to many top places at Charterhall, Errol and Crimmond during 1956. The present owner, Les Leach from Witney, discovered the little Rudge fairly recently. Sadly, though, the original engine and gearbox had been removed, and all that remained was the rolling chassis. Leach has since restored the bike to running condition, with another two valve engine and a gearbox, and is having a new engine built to the same specifications as the Horne-modified unit.

Remarkably, as late as 1954, Rudges were still proving to be competitive on short circuits. Gerry Turner and Eric Tinkler, on Pike Rudges, were often the principal 250cc protagonists at Brands Hatch, in the absence of John Surtees on the REG, of course. Gerry Turner was a draughtsman from Stanmore in Middlesex, and his interest in Rudges led him to the Pike brothers in nearby

Handwritten annotations:

STAN PIKE
1947 5th 65.86
1949 7th 6908

ROLAND PIKE

T.T.			ULSTER
1948	2nd	7186	1949 6th
1949	3rd	7280	
1950	4th	7414	
1951	R.		
1952	13th	7395	

T.T.	ULSTER
1947 Paddy Johnson 8th	Chris Tattersall was 7th in 1949 + 1950 and 9th 1952
1949 R Edwards 4th 6891	
1950 R Edwards 9th 6721	
1950 C. Tattersall 11th	

Jackie Horne
1954   10th 75.64 TT.
Also 5th in Ulster G.P.

Big Gerry Turner dwarfs his 250 Rudge at
Scarborough in 1954.

Gerry Turner's Pike Rudge, showing the
large TT carb, modified front brake, and
modified rear suspension.

Edgware. With help from Roland Pike, Gerry developed his 250 two valve Rudge into a very competitive machine. This machine had a home-made swinging arm conversion, similar to Roland Pike's machine, but it retained the girder forks. Gerry notched up three wins at Brands Hatch in 1954, and several second places to John Surtees on the REG, at Brands and Crystal Palace.

Excelsior Manxman

Though probably not as readily available as the Rudge, the Excelsior Manxman, by virtue of it's proven overhead camshaft engine, was also a very popular pre-war machine. One of the early post-war examples was raced by Doug Beasley, a motor engineer from Coventry, whose name would later become synonymous with 250cc Velocettes. The Beasley Excelsior had a modified flywheel assembly giving it a 'square' bore and stroke of 68 x 68mm. The engine and Albion close-ratio gearbox were mounted in a modified frame with swinging arm rear suspension and BSA telescopic forks. Riding his own machine, Doug was third in the 1948 Lightweight TT, at 67.68mph (108.2km/h). In 1950, the Beasley Excelsior underwent further modifications aimed at improving roadholding. The original frame was replaced by a light alloy duplex cradle frame with swinging arm rear suspension (built by Birmingham frame specialist Ernie Earles, whose skills in frame building and light alloy construction were very much in demand by the racing fraternity during the 1950s). Another popular modification to the Excelsior Manxman during the early 1950s, was to mount the engine in a Manx Norton plunger frame, and use a Norton gearbox, front forks, wheels and brakes. Excelsior enthusiasts Norman Webb and Charlie Brett, amongst others, rode similarly-modified machines.

The Hampshire-based company of Marsh and Fry, run by racing riders Reg Marsh and Frank Fry, also produced a Manxman-based Special known as the M&F Excelsior. It was originally ridden by Reg Marsh himself, who had a win at Blandford and a second place at Thruxton in 1950. The M&F later became more successful when it acquired a duplex cradle frame, swinging arm rear suspension and telescopic forks. Ridden mainly by Welshman, Ivor Lloyd, it was particularly successful between 1953 and 1955, at circuits such as Aberdare, Warminster and Ibsley, where it usually finished in the first three. It was later ridden by Ken James from the Isle of Wight, who raced it on short circuits and in the TT up to 1959. A similar machine was raced by John Eckart from Coventry. His Excelsior used the ex-Doug Beasley, all alloy works-type engine in a modernised swinging arm frame, but retained girder-type forks. With this essentially pre-war machine, Eckart dominated the 250cc class at Alton Towers between 1953 and 1955. Some of his more remarkable performances, against more modern machines, included a win at the Cadwell Park Championships in September 1954, two more wins in 1956 at Cadwell Park in April and August, and a win at Mallory Park in July.

The list of riders who raced Excelsiors during the late 1940s and early 1950s is a long one, and included such stalwarts as Ben Drinkwater, Les Martin, Norman Webb, Bill Maddrick and Jack Brett. Even after the Excelsiors had ceased to be competitive on English short circuits, they enjoyed something of a renaissance in Ireland where, ridden by the likes of Dave Andrews and Willie Ferguson, they continued to consistently win the 250cc class in the Irish classics until well into the 1950s.

Apart from the more popular Rudges and Excelsiors, the use of New Imperials and OK Supremes was not uncommon. Among the early exponents

T.T Excelsiors

1947. 3rd Ben Drinkwater 70·14
7th Sven Sorensen
9th Les Martin
10th Jack Brett.

1948 3rd Doug Beasley 67·78
6th Jackie McCredie

1949 5th Sven Sorensen 71·00

1950 7th Sven Sorensen 69·34
10th Norman Webb 65·26

1951 7th Sven Sorensen 70·89
9th Arnold Jones 68·25

1953. 8th Arnold Jones 72·26

13th 1958 TT 66·88 Clypse

Ulster G.P. Excelsiors

1949 D Beasley 5th, G Reeve 4th
1950 A Burton 4th
D Andrews 5th
W. Campbell 6th, N. Webb 7th
1951 N. Blemings 6th 75·32
1947 Les Martin 3rd 74·20
Jackie McCredie 2nd 65·52
H Kirby 3rd 7th 64·13
1954 D G Andrews 7
1952. D G Andrews 7th
T Sloan, 8th
J. McCredie 10th
1953. W. Ferguson 7th
S. Hodgins 9th
1954 D. G. Andrews 7th

11

Ron Mead on his modified New Imperial, in the 1948 Lightweight TT.

Doug Beasley on his modified Excelsior Manxman in the 1948 TT. 3rd 6768

A fairly original pre-war Excelsior Manxman ridden by Sven Sorensen in the 1948 TT.

The pre-war Excelsior Manxman was another popular machine during the early post-war period. (Courtesy Beaulieu Archives)

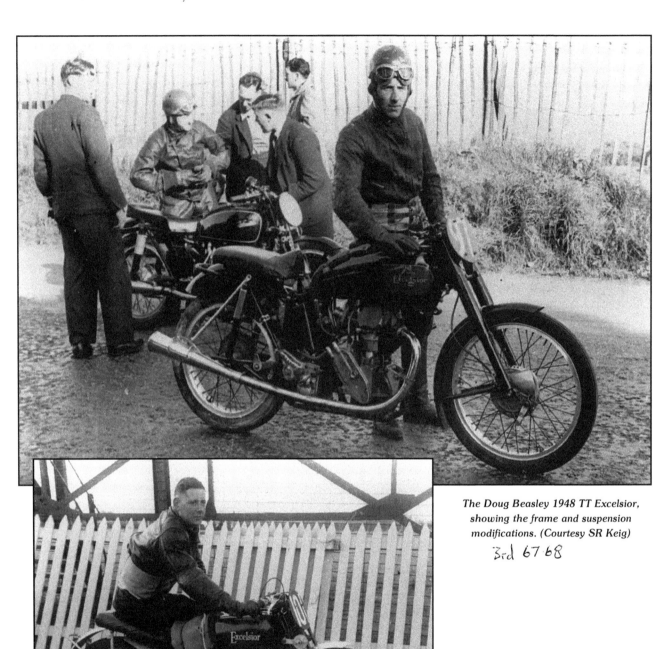

The Doug Beasley 1948 TT Excelsior, showing the frame and suspension modifications. (Courtesy SR Keig)

3rd 67 68

Norman Webb with his Excelsior Manxman at the TT in 1949. (Courtesey SR Keig)

The final version of Roland Pike's Rudge in 1950, with telescopic forks and experimental front brake. (Courtesy VMCC Archives)

One of the Rudge-based CTS Specials as used by Les Martin in the 1950 TT. (Courtesy SR Keig)

A modified OK Supreme, with swinging arm frame and Triumph gearbox, ridden by H Harrison in the 1951 TT. (Courtesy SR Keig)

14th
60:25

Another Excelsior Special, essentially a Manxman engine in a Manx Norton rolling chassis, used by Charlie Brett in the 1951 TT. (Courtesy SR Keig)

of New Imperials was Ray Petty, who finished fifth in the 1948 Lightweight TT on one. Ron Mead, a gifted engineer from Crewe in Cheshire, also raced a much-modified New Imperial in 1948.

Although the use of these pre-war racing machines was basically due to lack of choice, their suitability, performance and reliability was to some extent enhanced by the use of special fuels, such as Petrol/Benzole and Methanol, which were often permitted during the early post-war period. Even the important National Silverstone 'Saturday' meeting in 1950 was un-restricted. Although fuel restrictions began to be introduced in the 1950s, many minor meetings on the less popular circuits continued to be free from fuel restrictions, and one of the last un-restricted meetings was run at Brands Hatch as late as May 1952.

As well as the aforementioned pre-war racing machines, there were some post-war 250s, built using the humble pushrod engine, which proved quite successful. The MOV Velocette was one of the more commonly used, and several examples were raced in modified form during the 1950s. One of the early MOV exponents was Jim Hiscock, whose home-built Special proved successful during the pre-1950 period at the Altcar, Brough and Cadwell Park circuits.

Jackie Horne with his very pretty modernised Rudge, at the TT in 1954.
(Courtesy SR Keig) 10th

75.64

New Imperial TT
1949 4th Les Archer 6981
6th George Paterson 6849
1948 5th Ray Petty
1949 10th Ray Petty 6814

ART Velocette

By far the most successful MOV-based machine was the ART Velocette, developed by Shipston-on-Stour motorcycle dealer Arthur Taylor, and his chief mechanic Ted Clark. This very basic machine started life as a grass track machine, ridden by future World Champion Cecil Sandford in the early stages of his career. Around 1948, however, it was decided to convert the MOV for road racing. The engine already had a bronze head and hairpin valve springs, and an alloy Alfin barrel was turned out by Ted Clark in Taylor's workshop. Later, the bronze head was changed for a post-war MAC alloy head, modified to take hairpin valve springs. A TT carburettor and a megaphone exhaust system were fitted, and the bike was set up to run on a 50/50 mixture of Petrol and Benzole. The original lightweight-type gearbox, which contained a very unique set of non-standard close-ratio gears, was retained. These parts had been painstakingly selected from various models by factory parts wizard Bob Burgess. The standard rigid WD-type frame was used, but the girder forks were changed for Dowty telescopics.

Cecil Sandford would be the first to admit that the bike was functional rather than pretty, but it was light, handled well and was an easy starter. It was very good in short races, but in longer races it tended to overheat and the power dropped off. There is little doubt that the ART Velocette helped to establish Cecil's road racing career, and provided him with a long list of wins well into the 1950s.

Although a basic pushrod machine, the MOV often had the ability to humble more sophisticated machines. Cecil Sandford related a particular example: "I was due to ride one of the new Velocette works double overhead cam 250s at the Thruxton International meeting in August 1951. Arthur and I had taken the MOV with us just in case. It was a pretty awful wet day which made me realise that the works bike, with its narrow power band, would prove tricky to ride in the prevailing conditions. I therefore made the decision to ride the MOV instead. This did not please team manager Bertie Goodman. My decision proved to be correct, and I won the race fairly easily on the MOV, with my team mates Bob Foster and Bill Lomas second and third on the works bikes."

The little MOV continued to be successful until the end of 1953. By the standards of the day it was still a very basic machine, particularly with it's lack of rear suspension, but it provided Cecil Sandford with a win at the last Eppynt meeting, and several other places in national events, before being finally pensioned off at the end of 1953. It has now been completely restored by Bob Mallett, a former employee at AR Taylor Garages in Shipston-on-Stour, and returned to Cecil Sandford.

Les Diener Velocette

While the MOVs raced in Britain remained basic pushrod, overhead valve versions, the potential of the high camshaft design was exploited to the full by two engineers/riders, one in Australia and the other in South Africa. Australian Les Diener built his gear-driven, double overhead cam MOV in 1953. A casting attached to the top of the modified timing case carried the nine spur gears which drove the camshafts, and the camshaft housings were bolted to a modified MOV cylinder head with hairpin valve springs. The standard bore and stroke of 68 x 68mm was retained, and the engine and Velocette gearbox were mounted in a special duplex cradle frame with swinging arm rear suspension and BSA telescopic forks. Between 1954 and 1957, Les Diener notched up numerous

wins on the Eldee (as in LD, Les Diener) Velocette, which was reputed to be the fastest 250 in Australia at the time.

Cecil Sandford on the remarkably successful ART MOV Velocette, at Eppynt in 1953. (Courtesy VMCC Archives)

Jannie Stander Velocette

Jannie Stander, in South Africa, built a similar machine to that of Diener around the same time. Stander's slave engine was a 350 MAC, though, to which he fitted a new crankshaft assembly with outside flywheel to reduce the capacity to 250cc. The camshaft was driven by gears from the MOV timing chest. A KTT-type, close-ratio gearbox was used, and the frame was basically standard Velocette, with swinging arm rear suspension and Norton front forks. A characteristic of the machine was its very short exhaust pipe, and long, shallow-taper megaphone which extended beyond the rear wheel spindle. In 1953, Stander began to challenge the reigning Charlie McCullum-prepared

Australian Les Diener with his double overhead cam MOV Velocette in 1957. This picture shows the neat cam gear casting, and the duplex cradle frame.

Ron Jones on his Triumph Tiger 70 Special, winning the 250 race at the first televised road race meeting at Aberdare Park on June 18th 1955.

MOVs of Boet Ferreira and Eddie Grant, and over the next few years he scored numerous wins on his home-built machine, including the 1957 Port Elizabeth 200 mile handicap, where he beat Geoff Duke on a Gilera. He brought the Velocette with him to Europe in 1960, and raced it at Silverstone, Oulton Park and on the Continent, where it was not disgraced, despite being ridden against more modern and sophisticated machines.

Triumph Tiger 70

This was another popular machine in the 250cc class, and its engine formed the basis for several successful home-built Specials. Len Bayliss from Coventry, who worked as a road tester at the Triumph factory, used a modified Tiger 70 engine in his grass track cum road racing Elbee Specials, on which he was a consistent performer during the early 1950s, particularly at his local circuit of Ansty. In the 1950 Lightweight TT, Len finished a worthy fifth, at 71.53mph (114.48km/h). The Elbee engine used Excelsior flywheels and had a specially-made cylinder barrel. The standard cylinder head was converted to use hairpin valve springs. Around 1950, the engine was mounted in a duplex cradle frame, with McCandless swinging arm rear suspension.

*Len Bayliss, Elbee, TT
1949 8th 68.83
1950 5th 71.53*

Harry Pearce, another ex-grass track rider, also enjoyed success with a Tiger 70-based machine, particularly during the early days of road racing at Brands Hatch. In fact, Harry, riding his 250 Triumph, had the distinction of being the first rider to win a road race on the new Brands Hatch road circuit on 9th April 1950.

Another well-known 250 Triumph exponent was Wilmott Evans, who had a big alloy barrel Tiger 70. He won the first 250cc race at the Eppynt circuit in August 1948 on this machine, beating Maurice Cann's Guzzi. The Triumph engine was later mounted in a 7R AJS frame. Bill McVeigh also used a Tiger 70, and was very successful at the Cadwell Park circuit in the pre-1950 period.

A typical Tiger 70-based racer, and a perfect example of the way in which many Specials were created with limited resources, was the machine ridden by Welshman Ron Jones, who was particularly successful during the 1950s at Eppynt, Aberdare and Rhydymwyn. He bought his machine from Fron Purslow in 1951, when it already had an alloy cylinder head and barrel, components produced and sold by Wilmott Evans. It also had a post-war Triumph close-ratio gearbox, TT carb, and BTH racing magneto. BSA Gold Star forks and front brake replaced the original girder forks. The machine came with a very poor reputation for reliability, though, but over a period of time Ron Jones rectified the problems and developed the Triumph into a very competitive machine. During the winter of 1951/1952, the con rod and flywheels were polished, and the rockers were lightened and polished. A Tiger 100 'dope' piston was fitted with a $\frac{1}{8}$ inch (3.0mm) compression plate, which gave a compression ratio of 9:1, although still running on normal fuel. Various other minor modifications were made, such as fitting a front brake air scoop, and a rev counter drive.

In it's first race at Rhydymwyn in 1952, Ron finished third. In the quest for more speed, Ron cut the tops off the standard cams, welded them up and then reground them to give more lift and dwell. This pushed the revs up by nearly 800rpm, but caused a problem with broken valve springs. This was cured by fitting standard Triumph T70 Terrys valve springs, which pushed the maximum revs up to 7600rpm. The results of his efforts was a win at Eppynt on May 3rd. For 1953, Ron built a spring frame, using car steering columns as the main frame tubes, and Ford Popular radius rods for the swinging arm.

A typical Tiger 70 Triumph Special, with post-war forks, front brake, gearbox and sprung hub. (Courtesy VMCC Archives)

Len Bayliss on his Triumph T70 Elbee Special at Ansty, circa 1950.

Harry Pearce with his Triumph Special, setting a lap record on the Brands Hatch grass track in June 1949.

Harry Pearce with his beautifully-prepared Triumph converted for road racing, prior to the start of the 250 race which he won. This was the first Brands Hatch road race meeting, on 9th April 1950.

The M&F Excelsior with updated frame and telescopic front forks, ridden by Ken James in the 1957 Lightweight TT. (Courtesy Ken James)

R 1957
13ᵗ 1958   66.88
R 1959

The ex-John Eckart Excelsior Manxman, now with Earles forks and featherbed-type frame, as ridden by Jim Dakin, circa 1957.

The rear suspension units were the popular car-type Newton dampers, suitably modified. The entire frame was built at a cost of less than £5.00. Engine modifications included lightening the flywheels, by machining $1/8$ of an inch (3.0mm) off the rims.

At the last ever Eppynt meeting, on May 2nd 1953, the 250 race was won by Cecil Sandford on the Arthur Taylor MOV Velocette. Ron was pipped for second place by Fron Purslow on a Beasley Velocette, but the tables were turned later at Aberdare in August, when Ron won the 250 race from Brian Purslow on the Beasley Velocette. Development continued until 1956, by which time the increased power output was proving too much for the standard con rod, and a Gold Star rod was fitted with an eccentric big end sleeve to achieve the correct length and stroke. Ron's last race on the little Triumph was at Mallory Park in September 1956, after which the bike was sold back to Fron Purslow.

Lomas Enfield

One rather unlikely model which proved to be extremely successful was the 250 Royal Enfield built and raced by future World Champion Bill Lomas. This machine started life as a pre-war, overhead valve pushrod engine, in a rigid frame with telescopic forks. In 1948, it was given rear suspension, by mounting a Royal Enfield swinging arm between two large alloy plates attached to the rear part of the frame. These alloy plates also supported the Albion close-ratio racing gearbox. The engine had an alloy cylinder and a bronze cylinder head which had been modified to use hairpin valve springs, while the lubrication system was changed to dry sump. In this form, and running on ordinary pump fuel, the engine was producing 23bhp at 7800rpm. The development work on the machine was carried out by Bill Lomas in his home workshops, which were part of the family motorcycle business in Milford, Derbyshire.

Bill Lomas dominated the 250cc class at Cadwell Park during 1948 and 1949 on the Royal Enfield, winning the Cadwell 250 Championships three years running. During 1949, a second engine was built and converted to double overhead camshafts in order to exploit higher engine revs with greater reliability. The chain drive to the camshafts was taken from the inlet valve gear, and was housed in a one piece alloy case to which the two camboxes were bolted. The valves were operated by cam followers and coil springs. Although the conversion only yielded a very slight gain in power, it enabled the engine to be revved safely to 8500rpm. The 'double knocker' made its debut at Ansty on the 1st of April, where Bill finished second, but over the following Easter weekend he had a win at Brough on Good Friday and another win at Cadwell on Easter Monday. By now Bill had been recruited into the Velocette works team, and the 250 Enfield went into storage. Later, the pushrod engine was reinstalled and the machine was occasionally loaned out to other riders, including Derby veteran Alf Briggs, who had a third at Alton Towers in April 1957, followed by a second to Jack Murgatroyd's Beasley Velocette at Mallory Park on May 12th.

In the interests of historical accuracy, brief mention must be made of the two-stroke EMC machines fielded by Dr. Joe Ehrlich's company during 1947/1948. Although these machines did achieve some success, mostly when ridden by Les Archer Jnr., they were basically pre-war DKW racers, and do not really qualify as British-built machines.

Bill Lomas on his Royal Enfield Special with which he dominated the 250 class at Cadwell Park in the late 1940s.

The Lomas 250 Royal Enfield engine with double overhead cam conversion.

The Lomas Royal Enfield as it is today, with original pushrod engine installed.

A recent photograph of the restored 250 ART MOV Velocette.

Close up of the ART MOV showing engine and gearbox details.

The Horne Rudge in 2003, restored by Les Leach and temporarily fitted with a slave engine.

Chapter 2
The REG

The lack of a competitive, British-built post-war 250, had caused much comment in the motorcycling press during the late 1940s. Bob Geeson, an engineer from Ruislip in Middlesex, and who had raced at Brooklands before the war, was racing a home-modified, Rudge-based machine at the time, called the REG (for RE Geeson). Taking up the challenge thrown down by the motorcycling press, Bob Geeson decided to put his engineering skills to good use by building an all-new British 250cc machine from scratch. His first project involved collaboration with another engineer called Gordon Allen, from nearby Ealing in West London, who had designed and built the bottom half of a twin cylinder 250. To complete the engine, Bob designed and built a gear-driven twin overhead camshaft cylinder head assembly. The engine was duly completed and installed in Bob's original REG frame, but the Allen REG, as it was called, suffered from repeated big end failures during 1949, caused by a design fault in the crankshaft cum lubrication system. Bob, therefore, decided to build a completely new engine on his own.

Following a move to South Croydon, where he was employed as a Senior Production Engineer for the Metal Box company, Bob found himself with greater access to engineering resources. The crankshaft assembly was completely redesigned and, in his own home workshop, Bob turned out a one-piece Nitralloy crankshaft from a solid billet. The substantial crankshaft assembly had two small bob weights per cylinder, and was supported in the centre by a separate casting, into which the centre main bearing housing was bolted. Oil was fed directly to the big ends via the centre main bearing. The RR56 connecting rods had split bigend eyes which ran directly on the crankshaft, and an external flywheel was mounted on the drive side end, outside the engine sprocket. The drive to the twin overhead camshafts was taken from the right side of the crankshaft via a

Bob Geeson with his REG at the TT in 1952. (Courtesy SR Keig)

Timing side view of the REG, showing the large alloy casting which housed the gear train to the camshafts.
(Courtesy VMCC Archives)

Drive side view of the REG, showing the outside flywheel and primary drive. (Courtesy VMCC Archives)

train of gears to the inlet camshaft, with another idler gear driving the exhaust cam. An offset gear drove the magneto, and the drive gears were supported by roller bearings in an alloy outrigger plate. Specially-designed lightweight tappets actuated the valves, and coil valve springs were used.

A new cylinder head was machined from a blank magnesium alloy casting, and the cylinders were another one-piece alloy casting with pressed in liners. The bore and stroke were 54mm x 54mm, and the engine was designed to rev to 10,000rpm. It was mounted, together with an Albion racing gearbox, in the original Rudge/REG frame, with Norton front forks, AJS 7R front hub, and Dudley Ward swinging arm rear suspension.

Ridden by Bob in its TT debut in 1950, the REG may well have finished on the leader board had it not suffered a broken oil pipe which smothered the rear of the machine in oil. The subsequent lengthy pit stop to cure the problem dropped it down to twelfth place. Bob continued to race the REG over the next couple of years with some encouraging results, particularly at the Boreham airfield circuit where he had a second and a fifth place in 1951. In 1952, he had a fourth at the Silverstone 'Saturday' meeting, and fourth and sixth places again at Boreham. His TT efforts in 1951 and 1952 both ended in retirements, and in his last TT in 1953 he finally finished tenth. 7|74

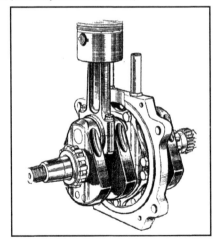

Technical drawing of the REG crankshaft assembly and centre main bearing housing.

30

Although the REG displayed great potential, it was often put out of action due to minor faults. One of its major problems was the lack of a magneto which could withstand its high revs. Both BTH and Lucas units had proved unsatisfactory and, in desperation, an Italian Scintilla unit was tried, as well as a coil and battery system.

Although Bob Geeson was a much better rider than most people were prepared to give him credit for, he was handicapped with mobility problems caused by an earlier accident injury, which got worse as time went on. He realised that the potential of the REG could be better exploited by a younger and fitter rider. In 1953, John Surtees was starting to establish his short circuit supremacy on a pair of featherbed Nortons. He accepted the offer of a ride on the REG at the Blandford International meeting in August, where he finished third behind the Moto Guzzis of Fergus Anderson and Maurice Cann. In the meantime, Bob Geeson himself demonstrated the REG's potential with a third at Castle Coombe on July 18th, and a second at Crystal Palace on August 2nd. Finally, though, it was John Surtees who gave the REG its first win, at Brands Hatch on September 27th.

In 1954, Bob finally reaped the rewards of his endeavours, when he engaged John Surtees to ride the REG on a regular basis. John recalls; "having already had a win on the superb little REG at Brands in September the previous year, my next ride on it was at the Silverstone 'Saturday' meeting in April, where the engine seized causing a lot of damage. Bob worked like a Trojan and rebuilt the engine in less than a week, for the Brands Good Friday meeting, where it ran beautifully and I won the 250 race from Benny Rood's Velocette." The REG won again at Crystal Palace on Easter Monday, where Surtees beat Maurice Cann's Guzzi and set a new 250 lap record of 69.31mph (110.89km/h). During that 1954 season, Surtees and the REG dominated the 250cc class, with four wins at Brands Hatch, two at Crystal Palace, one each at Cadwell Park and Castle Coombe, also establishing several new lap records. Just for good measure, Bob himself was second to Maurice Cann's Guzzi, and set a new lap record at Thruxton on June 7th, was second again at Silverstone on June 26th, and finished sixth in the Ulster Grand Prix. At the end of 1954, the REG was sold to Australian rider Jack Walters, who took it back to Australia. This gave Bob Geeson the means and the incentive to start work on a new version, with the added prospect of producing two complete machines.

The first Mark 2 REG was completed in 1956 and, to put things into their historical context, it must be remembered that, by now, opposition to the British machines in the 250cc class included the new Sportmax NSU, a couple of 203cc MVs, a Mondial, and the usual Guzzis. The latest REG engine incorporated several improvements, particularly to the valve gear and camshaft lubrication system. There was also a new semi-duplex cradle frame with a single braced top rail. Initially, Earles-type forks were fitted, but these were replaced by Norton Roadholders. The machine was finished off with a Moto Guzzi style full 'dustbin' fairing. By now, though, Bob's problems with his hip joint had forced him to retire from racing, and lightweight specialist Jim Baughn rode the Mark 2 on its debut. He later gave it its first win at the end of season Brands meeting on October 7th, beating Ian Clark on a GMV and Roy Mayhew on his ex-works Velocette.

John Hartle was signed up to ride the REG in 1957 and, during pre-season tests at the MIRA test track, the bike was timed at over 125mph (201km/h).

Bob Geeson REG
TT 1950 12th
1953 10th
Ulster 1951 7th
1953 10th
1954 6th

John Surtees (on the REG) winning at Brands Hatch on Good Friday, April 1954.

John Surtees taking his second Easter win on the REG at Crystal Palace in April 1954.

The season started well, with a second place and the fastest lap, behind Cecil Sandford's Mondial, at Oulton Park on April 2nd. But the decision to enter the Classic GPs proved to be a little over-ambitious. In the German GP at Hockenheim in May, the REG was quicker than the works MVs and Mondials during practice, but the race was run in very wet conditions, and water got into the ignition system causing a misfire, which dropped Hartle down to eighth place. At the TT, Hartle was a non-starter on the REG, having fallen off and injured himself in the Junior race. The run of bad luck continued at the Dutch TT, where Hartle fell off and the throttles stuck wide open, wrecking the engine. The Hartle/REG partnership came to an end at the Belgian GP, when Hartle accepted the offer of the works MV of Roberto Colombo who had been killed in a practice crash. Ironically, this MV was a new double overhead cam twin, very similar in concept to the REG. Derek Minter stepped in as rider towards the end of 1957, and finished fourth at Brands Hatch on October 13th, behind the 203 MVs of Mike O'Rourke and George Catlin, and Dan Shorey's Norvel.

The principal rider in 1958 was Derek Minter, who kicked off with a convincing win at Brands Hatch on Good Friday, beating Mike Hailwood's NSU. During the rest of the season, Derek's second and third places at Silverstone, Castle Coombe and Aintree, were extremely creditable, given the presence of Mike Hailwood and several other NSU-mounted riders. In the Isle of Man, the REG's TT jinx struck again resulting in a retirement for Derek Minter. On his own stamping ground at Brands Hatch on September 13th, Derek took the REG to another win, beating the ex-works 203 MVs of Dave Chadwick and Tom Thorp.

Despite his health problems and limited resources, Bob Geeson produced a second Mark 2 model in 1959. Derek Minter was still the principal rider for some of the more important events and the TT. Despite coming under increasing pressure from the foreign machines, Derek still managed to achieve some commendable rostrum places at Brands Hatch, the Blandford International, Silverstone 'Saturday' and Snetterton, but was a non-finisher again in the TT.

The sight of Derek Minter and Bob Anderson on two of his machines in the Hutchinson 100 at Silverstone, must have given Bob Geeson a great deal of satisfaction, though. Of the two riders, Derek Minter was best with a fifth place, headed mainly by Mondials and NSUs. Bob Anderson faired better later in the season, with a win at Brands on September 20th, and a fifth in the Aintree International on September 26th. Ginger Payne also shared one of the REGs and had a win at Brands in July, and second places at Biggin Hill, Castle Coombe and at the end of season Brands meeting in October, where he was second to Hailwood's Mondial, ahead of Fred Hardy and Dickie Dale on NSUs.

Bob Geeson persevered with the REG into the 1960s, when it was ridden by several riders, including Norman Surtees, Sid Mizen and Ray Fay. Sid Mizen rode it in the TT in 1960 and 1961 but retired on both occasions. In a one-off ride, Ray Fay had a win at Aintree in May 1961. It was Fred Hardy, however, whose name is inevitably linked with the REG's final years. An excellent rider/engineer himself, who had successfully raced his own home-built 250 NSU, Fred carried out much of the development work and preparation on the REG during 1961 and 1962. The final version could be identified by the external pipes on the cam gear outer cover and cam box, which fed oil to the camshafts and valve gear. The latest frame was a spine-type frame, with a large diameter top tube and vertical rear tube, joined by duplex tubes from below the steering head which ran under the engine to the swinging arm mounting. The swinging arm itself was square section. Improvements to the valve gear had pushed maximum revs up to 11,000rpm, while experiments continued to find an ignition system capable of sustaining these engine speeds. In a conversation with Fred Hardy, he confirmed that one other problem with the REG was its tendency to destroy primary chains in long races such as the TT. In fact, when Fred recorded the REG's best TT result with a seventh place in 1962, he started the race with the primary chain so deliberately slack that it was almost in danger of jumping off the sprockets, and there were hardly any rollers left on the chain at the finish!

Despite increased opposition from new foreign machines, Fred Hardy achieved some commendable results and occasional rostrum places at Brands Hatch, Crystal Palace and Aberdare Park. To his credit also goes the REG's final win when, on the long circuit at Brands Hatch on October 14th 1962, he beat Norman Surtees and Chris Vincent on the latest Aermacchis. Sadly, Fred Hardy passed away in November 2003 at the age of only 69. The last person to ride the REG was Chris Vincent, who rode it in its last race in the 1963 TT when, unfortunately, the ever-present ignition problems caused its retirement. Regretably, these remarkable machines suffered an unfortunate fate. One of the Mark 2 versions was sold and taken to Australia, and the whereabouts of this and the original Mark 1 is not known. The surviving UK machine was broken up, and only its engine is thought to have survived. Rumours have been rife that John Surtees was attempting to restore a complete machine, but to date there has been no reliable information on this project.

When Bob Geeson's high-revving, double overhead cam, twin cylinder machine appeared in 1950, the pinnacle of British motorcycle racing technology, was based on pre-war single cylinder designs. With the benefit of hindsight; the REG was way ahead of its time. This is borne out by the later evolution of successful machines based on the same concept. Machines such as the NSU Rennmax, the 250 MV twin, the 125 Gilera twin, and so on, right up to the 1960s 125 Honda twin, the 250 Jawa and CZ, the Bianchi and the Paton. Such comparisons only serve to reinforce the view that Bob Geeson must surely go down in motorcycle racing history as the most successful independent designer/builder of the 1950s. The fact that he never received any assistance from an apathetic British motorcycle industry is deplorable. One can only speculate as to what might have been achieved had he been given even a modicum of support from a British motorcycle manufacturer.

Chapter 3
OHC Nortons & Velocettes

Ron Mead

Inevitably, the limitations of the pre-war machines and the lack of spares to keep them running, led to the use of suitably-modified Manx Norton and KTT Velocette engines (reduced to 250cc, of course). One of the first of these successful hybrids, built by Ron Mead, a gifted engineer from Crewe in Cheshire, appeared in 1949. His 250 Norton had a bore and stroke of 70.5 x 67mm, used Excelsior flywheels in Norton crankcases, a Velocette con-rod and bigend, and a Norton cylinder head incorporating an ex-Maurice Cann double overhead camshaft conversion. The engine was mounted in a pre-war plunger Manx Norton frame with girder forks, and Norton wheels and brakes. Ron won the 250 Leinster 200 on this machine, finished fourth in the 1949 Lightweight TT, at 71.6mph (115.2km/h), and was third in the Ulster Grand Prix. In 1950, Ron Mead produced a 250cc Velocette which had a bore and stroke of 68 x 68.5mm, but appeared to be a standard KTT in all other respects. He won the 250 North West 200 on the Velocette, and finished third in the Lightweight TT. The original Mead Norton was later raced by both Fron and Brian Purslow during 1951/1952, when Ron Mead was working for Fron Purslow at the latter's Shrewsbury motorcycle dealership.

Keys Norton

Another early 250 Norton exponent was Basil Keys from Worthing in West Sussex, whose Norton appeared around the same time as that of Ron Mead. The technical details of this engine have proved difficult to trace, but evidence seems to suggest that it was a sleeved down, 350cc long stroke Manx Norton engine. The Keys Special, sometimes referred to as the BEK (after the initials BE Keys), was initially raced in fairly basic pre-war form using standard Norton

Ron Mead with his original double overhead cam 250 Norton at the TT in 1949. (Courtesy SR Keig)

4ᵗʰ 71·60

12ᵗʰ 66·97

Basil Keys with his 250 Norton at the TT in 1951. (Courtesy SR Keig)

Les Graham on one of the 1951
ex-works 250 Velocettes with the special
girder forks, seen here in the 1952 TT.
4th 82·06

Les Graham on his ex-works, 1951 250
'double knocker' Velo in the British
Championships at Boreham in August
1952. (Courtesy Beaulieu Archives)

12th, 1951 T.T

components, such as gearbox, frame, wheels and brakes. By 1951, though, it had been updated, when the engine and gearbox were mounted in an AMC swinging arm frame, with BSA Gold Star front forks and front wheel. Basil remained a worthy contender in the 250cc class until the late 1950s on his Norton, and was particularly successful at Blandford, Thruxton, Ibsley and Boreham, where he frequently achieved rostrum places.

Velocette

In 1951, Velocette became the only British factory to build a new 250cc racing machine. The new, double overhead camshaft engines followed normal Velocette practice, with 68 x 68.5mm bore and stroke, Alfin barrels and magnesium crankcases. The frames were modified Mark 8 units, with twin top rails and a central bracing tube, while the old girder forks were replaced with new, oil-damped telescopic forks which carried the front wheel spindle forward of the fork legs. New five speed gearboxes were fitted, early in the new racing season, to overcome the problems of a narrow power band. Grand Prix results with the new machines proved to be disappointing, though. Riding one of the early four speed versions, Cecil Sandford was fifth in the Swiss Grand Prix in May, Bob Foster retired the only model in the Lightweight TT, and Bill Lomas finished fifth in the French GP at Albi. At the end of season Hutchinson 100 at Silverstone in October, Bill Lomas eventually pulled off a consolation win. The new 250s had not lived up to expectations and Velocette virtually quit racing at the end of 1951. However, one of the five speed 250s was loaned to Les Graham in 1952. The previous year's telescopic forks were replaced by girder forks mounted on needle roller bearings, with an hydraulic damper inside the main spring. An experimental large diameter front brake with vane-type extractors was also fitted. Les Graham finished a worthy fourth in the Lightweight TT using this machine, behind three works Moto Guzzis. He was also third in the Ulster Grand Prix, and had a win at the Hutchinson 100 in September.

1951

Swiss GP, 5th Cecil Sandford
TT, 5th Arthur Wheeler 75·11
French GP. 5th Bill Lomas
Ulster GP 3rd Arthur Wheeler 83.00
          5th Doug Beasley 7795

8206

84·21

By now, more people had begun to turn their attention to the Manx Norton and KTT Velocette engines as more suitable power units for their Specials. The success of Ron Mead's Velocette in 1950 prompted many people to use similarly-modified KTT engines. Among them was Arthur Wheeler, the well-known motorcycle dealer from Epsom, who used a Mead engine in his 250 KTT in 1951, winning his class in the Leinster 100 and the North West 200, scoring a win at Blandford, and finishing fifth in the Lightweight TT. 75·11

Wheeler was 3rd in 1951 Ulster
@ 83·00 behind Bruno Ruffo and
Maurice Cann, Moto Guzzis. Also 7th SB Italian
Bill Webster was 5th in 1952 Dutch TT
9th 53 TT 71·96   6th in 1955 TT Clypse
14th 54 TT. 72.98
Sammy Hodgins was 6th on a Velo
                in the 1957 Ulster

Percy Tait was 8th in 1955 Ulster
                on a Velo
   H. Kirby was 10th on a Velo
L. Williams was 8th in 1951 Ulster
                on a Velo.

Doug Beasley

The best known 250cc Velocette exponent, however, was Doug Beasley, who collaborated with Ron Mead in building the first Beasley Velocette, which Ron rode in the 1951 TT. The Beasley engines had a modified flywheel assembly and connecting rod, designed to produce a square bore and stroke of 68 x 68.5mm, with the cylinder head re-machined to suit. The Velocette gearbox was retained, but new duplex cradle frames with swinging arm rear suspension were built. Various front forks were used, including Norton Roadholders, Earles-type, and the characteristic Velocette telescopic type, with the lower ends reversed to provide a trailing wheel spindle. When ill health eventually forced Doug to give up racing, his superbly turned out machines achieved success in the hands of riders such as Cecil Sandford, Bill Lomas and Percy Tait. A total of 11 Beasley Velocettes are thought to have been built, each with a slightly

Doug Beasley with his first 250 Velo at the TT in 1952. (Courtesy SR Keig)

Retired

Ray Petty at the TT in 1952, on his beautifully-prepared 250 Norton. (Courtesy SR Keig)

1952, 8ᵗʰ 7609
1953, 7ᵗʰ 7467
1954, 9ᵗʰ 7636

39

different specification, and each engine was numbered with an identifying DB prefix. Several examples are known to still exist in private collections.

Petty Norton

The use of Norton engines was also becoming popular by the early 1950s, and one of the neatest and best turned out 250 Nortons at the time was built by Ray Petty in 1952. Ray's own Manx Norton engine had been modified to an unusual bore and stroke of 64 x 77mm, and a capacity of 247cc. The engine and early upright-type gearbox were mounted in a scaled-down 'featherbed' frame, with Norton forks, wheels and brakes. This machine bore the hallmarks of Ray's meticulous attention to detail, which included a lower and lighter hand-built fuel tank, and a lightened front hub and brake plate. Later additions included a racing seat incorporating a small tail fairing. A neat handlebar cowl and front number plate assembly with an integral beak front mudguard, blended with alloy side panels and fully enclosed the engine. This made it one of the first fully-faired machines to be seen on British circuits. On its TT debut in 1952, Ray finished eighth and, in 1953, he finished seventh, at 74.67mph (120.14km/h), which compares favourably with the first privately-owned Guzzi of Arthur Wheeler which finished fourth at 80.38mph (129.3km/h). In May 1953, Ray also had a win at Blandford.

When he retired from racing, Ray set up his own business in Farnborough preparing Manx Norton engines. In addition to his original machine, Ray Petty built a total of six 250cc Norton engines, of which only two were built up as complete machines. One of the engines was loaned to the Cooper Car Company which used it to establish some world records with a Cooper car at Monza in 1957.

The original Petty Norton later passed into the hands of Shrewsbury racing dealer Fron Purslow. Fron had been a 250cc specialist since the early post-war days, and had raced a variety of British Specials, including BSAs, the aforementioned Mead Norton, and the Earles frame, ex-Lomas Beasley Velocette. The fate of the original 250 Petty Norton is unknown but, in 1960, Ray built a complete machine for John Bacon, with a 65 x 75mm bore and stroke, on which he finished twelfth in the Lightweight TT. John Williams also raced a 250 Petty Norton (which may have been the ex-John Bacon machine), early in his career in 1961/1962. The only known surviving 250 Petty Norton was built by Ray in 1984, for Tony Horn from Berkshire, using the ex-John Bacon engine and a replica frame built by Ken Sprayson.

A survey of the 250cc class entries for the two international meetings at Silverstone in 1952, shows that just over 50% were still basically British pre-war machines. With the exception of three foreign machines, the rest were either Velocette or Norton hybrids, reflecting the growing popularity of these machines.

Benny Rood Velocette

Another successful rider/engineer to appear about this time was Benny Rood. Having raced a Ron Mead Velocette in 1951, Benny set about building his own machine for 1952. KTT crankcases housed a modified flywheel assembly with the stroke shortened to 68.5mm (for which a shorter connecting rod had to be made). A blank KTT cylinder head was acquired, and Ron Mead filled and re-machined the combustion chamber to suit the 68mm bore. The Velocette gearbox was retained, and the engine was fitted into a semi-duplex cradle frame

Ray Petty , Petty Norton
1952 8th 76.09
1953 7th 74.67
1954 9th 76.36

NB He was
5th in 1948
10th in 1949
on New Imperial

6th in the Ulster 1952
on Petty Norton

Ray Petty on his Norton, winning the 250 race at Blandford on Whit Monday, 1953. (Courtesy Gordon Francis)

Fron Purslow on the Beasley/Earles Velo at Eppynt in 1953. (Courtesy VMCC Archives)

with a single top tube. Amazingly, Benny had built the frame without the aid of a tube bending machine!

A welded-up sub-frame carried the rear suspension units for the swinging arm. The front forks were a mixture of Matchless and BSA components, supported in a home-made bottom yolk and a fabricated alloy fork crown. KTT brakes and hubs were used front and rear, and the gearbox was a standard KTT. No mean rider himself, Benny took the Velocette to a win at the Silverstone Trophy day meeting, and also scored some impressive second places behind Maurice Cann's Guzzi at Thruxton, Boreham and Castle Coombe. In its second season, the Rood Velocette was easily the most successful British machine, with wins at Silverstone, Crystal Palace and Snetterton, plus some second places to Maurice Cann's Guzzi. In the Isle of Man, it was timed at just over 96mph (155.0km/h) down the Sulby straight during TT practice, but unfortunately retired in the race with a mechanical problem.

Ben Rood was 5th in the 1952 250cc Ulster GP on his Velo. 79.72

Beasley/Earles Velocette

Doug Beasley produced another of his Specials for Bill Lomas to ride in the 1952 TT. This had an Ernie Earles duplex cradle frame with crossed-over steering head tubes and an Earles front fork. A reduction in height of the new 68 x 68.5mm engine had been achieved by using a hand-forged, shortened connecting rod, which required steps to be machined in the flywheels to obtain the necessary piston skirt clearance at the bottom of the stroke. The cylinder head was a re-machined KTT component. This machine's TT debut was marred by a retirement, in what was probably Bill Lomas' only ride on it. It proved to be more successful in 1953, though, when Fron Purslow was third in the North West 200 and at Scarborough, and also had a couple of second places at Eppynt and Aberdare.

Over the next three or four years, the popularity of the Norton- and Velocette-based machines increased, and several dozen examples were built and raced. Many of them owed their origins to either Ron Mead or Doug Beasley, but as machines changed hands and reappeared in slightly different form, their origins became more difficult to trace.

Of the two power units, the Velocette appeared to be more popular, probably due to the fact that most of the KTT Velocettes had by now been replaced by the Featherbed Norton and the 7R AJS in the 350cc class. Many of the Norton engines being converted were based on the early long stroke, single overhead cam units.

Although the Norton/Velocette power units were often described as 'sleeved down', in fact, nearly all of them underwent a change of bore and stroke, the most popular dimensions being 68 x 68.5mm (particularly in the case of the Velocette engines), and was probably governed by the availability of suitable pistons. The choice of frames also varied a great deal. The Norton 'featherbed' frame was popular despite the fact that it was probably a bit too heavy for a 250cc machine. Some builders used proprietary frames built by specialists such as Ernie Earles or Charlie Lucas, while others built their own frames, which were usually modified versions of the ubiquitous Norton 'featherbed'. In 1953, British machines still made up over 90% of the entry in the 250cc class.

RDS (Reg Dearden Special) Norton

Manchester motorcycle dealer and well known TT entrant Reg Dearden also fielded a couple of interesting machines. One was the RDS, which was based on the bottom half of a pre-war 'works' Norton engine. This featured a new forged flywheel assembly, which had an integral drive side mainshaft and crankpin, and a new EN24 steel connecting rod. The cylinder head and barrel were re-machined to suit the new 68 x 68mm bore and stroke. A double knocker cam box and a 1³/₈ inch (35mm) GP carburettor was fitted, and coil ignition was used. The engine and four speed Norton gearbox were mounted in a scaled-down Reynolds 531 'featherbed' frame, with shortened Norton forks. Eric Houseley rode it in the TT in 1953, when it failed to finish, but he had a win on it at Scarborough in July.

Sid Willis Velocette

Over the years, and probably due to their isolation from the manufacturing base in the west, the Australians had proved to be extremely innovative in creating competitive racing machines. Sid Willis from Sydney was a typical example. He had successfully raced a pre-war, rigid frame, KTT Velocette, which had been sleeved down to 250cc, since 1946. To improve performance, it was fitted with an ex-works, double overhead cam cylinder head and cam box. These items had been purchased from a cache of factory racing spares that had been taken to Australia by legendary pre-war TT rider Frank Mussett. In 1953, Sid arrived in Europe to race on the Continent and in the TT. Experience on the Continent had shown up the limitations of his basic pre-war machine, so Sid purchased one of Doug Beasley's duplex cradle frames with Velocette front forks for the TT. With his own engine and gearbox installed, Sid finished a brave fifth in the Lightweight TT, behind Continental works machines and Arthur Wheeler's private Moto Guzzi. After his return to Australia at the end of the 1953 European season, he continued to be virtually unbeatable on his 250 Velocette in his home state of New South Wales for several more years.

Sid Willis Velocette
1952 TT 5ᵗʰ 75.38
1953 German 8ᵗʰ
GP at Solitude

75.38

The MELEM

Raced by Dudley Edlin from Uxbridge, Middlesex, the MELEM was another interesting mixture of Norton and Velocette components. Built in 1953, it consisted of the original ex-Ron Mead, ex-Fron Purslow 250 double overhead cam Norton engine, in a featherbed-type frame built by Charlie Lucas of Watford. An Albion gearbox was used, and the first version had Earles forks, though these were later replaced by Norton Roadholders. It also had a Manx Norton front wheel and brake. A distinguishing feature of the machine was its left hand side mounted exhaust system. During TT practice in 1954, the MELEM was timed at 93.28mph (150.08km/h) down the Sulby straight, and finished thirteenth in the race at 73.01mph (117.4km/h). Incidentally, MELEM was an amalgamation of the names of the people involved in its construction: Mead, Edlin, Lucas, Earles and Marley.

Dudley Edlin MELEM
1954 TT. 13ᵗʰ 73.01

Charlie Lucas was also responsible for producing a handful of Lucas Specials, using frames of his own design and 'cut-down' Velocette engines. One of these Velocettes was ridden quite successfully by Eric Pantlin. Doug Beasley had also handed over the riding of one of his Velocettes to local Coventry man Percy Tait, who started to achieve some favourable results on it in 1954. Another version was loaned to Cecil Sandford, who took it to second place behind Maurice Cann's Guzzi at the 'Silverstone Saturday' meeting in April. At the International Hutchinson 100 meeting, also at Silverstone in August, Cecil Sandford finished third in the first 250 race, and then, taking advantage of his uncanny wet weather ability, he scored a remarkable win in the 250

The 1953 ex-Reg Dearden 250 Norton a recent Mallory Park Vintage meeting. The rider is present owner, Phil Moss from Ledbury.

Dudley Edlin on the MELEM, with Earles forks, at Brands Hatch in June 1953.

Dudley Edlin's MELEM Special, which used the ex-Ron Mead double overhead cam Norton engine and Albion gearbox, in a special Lucas frame, seen here at the TT in 1954 with Norton forks and front wheel. (Courtesy SR Keig)

13ᴴ 73·01

Frank Cope on the original version of the 250 Norton at the TT in 1954.

45

The ex-Reg Dearden 250 Velo, with
ex-works five speed gearbox, ridden by
Eric Houseley in the 1954 TT.
(Courtesy SR Keig)

8th 77.17

Cecil Sandford on a Beasley Velocette in
1954. Although much of the technical
detail is obscured, the twin front down
tubes of the duplex frame and the
Velocette forks and front brake are clearly
visible. (Courtesy Cecil Sandford)

Veteran Basil Keys at Ibsley in 1954, on his updated Norton with AMC frame, BSA Gold Star forks and front wheel.
(Courtesy Gordon Francis)

Benny Rood's 1954 double overhead cam 250 Velo.

Benny Rood on his Velo at Brands Hatch on Good Friday 1954. Rood finished second to John Surtees on the REG. (Courtesy VMCC Archives)

Championship race. Cecil recalls; "there was a downpour just before the start of the race, and the track was awash in places. Racing in the wet never used to bother me very much, and after four laps I had built up a good lead when the engine suddenly cut out at Copse corner. I stopped and had a look at it, but could not find the cause. I had to give it a very long push to get it restarted and by now quite a few riders had gone past, including second man Arthur Wheeler on his Guzzi. Fortunately, it was a 20 lap race, and by making a real effort I caught and passed Arthur Wheeler a few laps from the finish to win fairly comfortably."

Benny Rood was also still very much in the picture in 1954. His 250 Velocette now featured his own double overhead camshaft conversion. This consisted of a cam box cast in Y alloy, which contained the gear train driving the camshaft gears, via idler gears, from the main vertical shaft drive pinion. The camshafts were supported in ball bearings, and the cam box was split vertically, while each camshaft gear had its own inspection cover, to permit vernier adjustments to the valve timing. Exposed hairpin valve springs were used, and the engine would rev safely to 9000rpm. Benny later went on to become one of the co-founders of Cosworth Engineering, and was directly involved in the design and development of the Formula One Grand Prix engines.

RDS (Reg Dearden Special) Velocette

Reg Dearden fielded two very similar hybrid Velocettes in 1954. These were also called RDS, and were allegedly the unsuccessful 1951 ex-works machines which had been used by Les Graham in 1952. While the source of these two machines must remain a mystery, it's well known that Reg was very much involved with Les Graham's racing activities on Velocettes in 1951 and 1952. One of the Dearden Specials was used by Eric Houseley, who rode it into eighth place in the TT. The girder forks with hydraulic dampers favoured by Graham had been replaced by a set of later telescopic forks with offset wheel spindle and, although it certainly had one of the five speed gearboxes, whether it had one of the double overhead cam engines has not been confirmed.

8th 7717.

To confuse things even more, Reg Dearden also provided another 250 Velocette, allegedly the second ex-works double overhead cam, five speeder, for the up-and-coming Manchester rider Dave Chadwick, who had some impressive results on it, including a win at Scarborough in July, and a second to Karl Lottes' DKW at the September International meeting. The fact that Eric Housely was sixth on the sister machine at Scarborough in July, confirms the existence of the two Dearden machines. Unfortunately, the passage of time has made it difficult to confirm the exact specifications and origins of these two machines. Furthermore, Reg Dearden's machines were usually dismantled when not in use, and he was well known for swapping around engines and frames amongst his vast collection of machines, which only adds to the confusion.

Dave Chadwick was 5th 1955 TT. Clypse 64:20

IFT (Ian F Telfer) Norton

Among the new Nortons to appear in 1954 was the 250 IFT built by Ian Telfer, an engineering draughtsman from Harrow Weald in Middlesex. Ian had been racing his own home-built 250 Specials since 1948, based at first on the MOV Velocette and later a KSS version. His Norton was based on an ex-Arthur Fenn 1950 long stroke 350 Manx. The flywheels were re-machined and the stroke reduced to 68mm, while an alloy con rod and a 68mm Martlett piston were used to bring the capacity down to 250cc. The cylinder head was completely re-worked by Ron Mead to suit the 250cc cylinder. The engine, together with an older-type upright Manx gearbox, was mounted in a standard Norton 'featherbed' frame acquired from Francis Beart, with Norton forks, wheels and brakes. John Surtees rode this machine for the first time at Ibsley in August 1954, when he finished second, and later scored two wins on it at Aberdare on August 28th and Brands Hatch on September 12th.

Ian Telfer was 10th in the 1954 Ulster GP

Cope Norton

Another interesting Norton that appeared in 1954 was ridden by veteran Birmingham motorcycle dealer Frank Cope, who had previously campaigned a sleeved down 250cc 7R AJS. The Cope Norton was allegedly based on an experimental ex-works, over-square, outside flywheel 350cc engine. The capacity was reduced to 250cc by sleeving the bore down to 66mm, later changed to 65mm, with an altered stroke of 72mm. The engine was mounted in a standard 'featherbed' Manx Norton frame. Later in its life, an experimental ex-works, AMC-type five speed gearbox was fitted, and the cylinder head was changed to a later type with the splined camshaft drive. The standard Manx frame was lowered and the Norton Roadholder forks were replaced by the Ken Sprayson-designed Reynold's leading link front fork. It was ridden mainly

5566 (last) Clypse

in the TT until 1958, when its best performance was ninth place in 1956; after which it went to South Africa, where Frank raced it successfully for a few years. Fortunately, this historic machine has now been returned to England, and has been completely restored to working order by historic racing enthusiast Harry Whitehouse.

NSU Sportmax

In 1955, the German NSU company produced the single cylinder, single overhead camshaft Sportmax racer, based on its road going 250cc model. This became the first post-war production 250cc racing machine to go on sale, but was only produced in limited numbers. John Surtees took delivery of one of the first machines in the UK, and another Sportmax was acquired by Irish sponsor Terry Hill for Sammy Miller. This proved to be a turning point in the hitherto British monopoly of the 250cc class. To add weight to the Continental opposition, long term Moto Guzzi specialists Arthur Wheeler and Maurice Cann were joined by Cecil Sandford on a 1954 ex-works machine. Consequently, the British-built machines were now finding it difficult to get into the first three places at most National meetings.

GMV (Geoff Monty Velocette)

Among the more successful British machines in 1955, was the GMV built by Twickenham-based racing dealer Geoff Monty. Geoff had been racing since 1947, and from very early on he developed a flair for building hybrids. One of the first Geoff Monty Specials was a 7R AJS, married up to a Norton gearbox and mounted in a lightweight frame which he'd designed and built himself in the early 1950s. The famous race shop of Monty and Ward, opposite Twickenham Green in Southwest London, became something of a Mecca for racing enthusiasts in the 1950s, and over the years Geoff and Allan Dudley-Ward provided racing machines for many well-known riders, such as Bob Anderson, Alan Shepherd, Tommy Robb, Ron Langston, Bill Ivy and Dave Degens.

The first 250 Geoff Monty Velocette appeared at Silverstone in April 1954, where Geoff finished fourth in the 250 race. He finished third at Thruxton in June. The GMV was based on a Velocette Mark 8 KTT engine, which retained the original bore of 74mm, but had a modified flywheel assembly with a stroke of 58mm. To accommodate the ultra short stroke, the connecting rod was shortened by cutting and rewelding. The cylinder head remained basically 350 KTT in respect of valve sizes and combustion chamber, with a standard KTT camshaft and carburettor. Ignition was by 6 volt battery and coil, and the gearbox was also a KTT component. A modified 'featherbed' frame was used, with Norton forks, wheels and brakes. Geoff gave the GMV its first win at Thruxton on April 11th 1955, and also recorded several noteworthy second and third places on it at Brands Hatch, Blandford, Oulton Park and Ibsley.

A total of four GMVs, including the prototype, are thought to have been built by Geoff Monty. One of the first machines was purchased by Dick Harding for the 1956 season, during which he had wins at Brands Hatch and Aberdare, plus several other rostrum places. Another machine was built in 1956 for Peter Chatterton, and a third machine was built for Dennis Pratt to race in 1957. The original prototype model was purchased by Jervis Hyde in 1956.

Meanwhile, Reg Dearden had installed one of the ex-works Velocette, five speed twin cam engines into a featherbed-type frame, to create another

Ian Telfer's IFT Norton ridden by John
Surtees at Ibsley in August 1954.
(Courtesy Gordon Francis)

Ian Telfer on a slightly later version of his
IFT Norton, with a later type gearbox, at
Scarborough in 1955.
(Courtesy Gordon Francis)

Taken at the Hutchinson 100 in 1955, this picture clearly illustrates the extent of British machine involvement in the 250cc class in the 1950s. Of the 24 machines, 17 are British Specials. 35. John Hogan (British Anzani) 18. LR King (JEL) 11. Geoff Monty (GMV) 8. Tom Thorp (BSA) 34. H Kirby (Beasley Velocette) 1. Don Whelan (Beasley Velocette) behind him is Ted Kempson (Rudge) 19. FL Fuller (Rudge) 37. GA Coulter (Rudge) 23. C Ellerby (AJS) 40. Basil Keys (Norton) 6. Eric Pantlin (Lucas Special) 20. John Patrick (MOV Velocette) 4. Jervis Hyde (Rudge) 32. Howard German (Duffell Velocette) 24 Phil Carter (IFT Norton) 26. Dudley Edlin (MELEM). The other machines are 22. Race winner Arthur Wheeler (Moto Guzzi) 27. Karl Lottes (DKW) 33. Jim Baughn (EMC Puch) 9. Bill Webster (MV) 29. John Surtees (NSU) 38. Cecil Sandford (Moto Guzzi) 10. Unidentified rider on a Continental machine. (Courtesy Mortons archive)

Geoff Monty on the GMV with full 'dustbin' fairing (Thruxton or Ibsley, circa 1955).

A typical 1950s Anglo/Italian battle. Geoff Monty (GMV) leading the Moto Guzzis of Arthur Wheeler and Maurice Cann at Silverstone, probably 1954.

Mike O'Rourke on the Geoff Monty
Velocette, at Brands Hatch in 1955.

A right hand side view of the GMV. This is
the prototype model raced by Jervis Hyde
in 1957.

1955 Chadwick 5th £420)
Carter 7th 60.01) Clypse

version of the RDS, on which Dave Chadwick scored wins in the Southern 100, Oulton Park, and Altcar, as well as a fifth place in the Lightweight TT. To add to the confusion, Reg also re-introduced the Norton-powered RDS on which Phil Carter finished seventh in the Lightweight TT. Fortunately, the Norton RDS remained virtually intact, and reappeared in Classic Racing in the 1980s ridden by its current owner Phil Moss from Ledbury.

By 1955, Ian Telfer's IFT Norton had undergone further modification, to over-square dimensions of 71 x 62.5mm, using a new one piece crankshaft assembly consisting of the crankpin, flywheel and drive side mainshaft. A steel con rod in EN24 was used which pushed the safe rpm up to 8200, and in this form the engine was producing about 28bhp. The old pre-war, upright Manx gearbox had also been changed for one of the latest type. The rather studious looking but extremely capable Phil Carter from Northwich in Cheshire, rode the IFT into seventh place in the TT, after a pit stop to cure a clutch problem, and later had a second place at Oulton Park in July, behind Dave Chadwick on the RDS, and a sixth at the Hutchinson 100 meeting. Ian himself rode it to second place, behind Cecil Sandford's Guzzi, at the Scarborough International meeting in September. Some of the other well known riders who raced the IFT Norton were Cecil Sandford, who had two third places behind the NSUs of Surtees and Miller at the very wet Silverstone 'Saturday' meeting in April 1956, and Terry Shepherd, who had an end of 1956 season win at Mallory Park. The last person to ride the IFT for Ian Telfer was John Clark, who rode it in the 1957 TT, after which the machine was sold to Peter Doncaster.

Even more Continental machines began to appear in British events in 1956, and several other riders had acquired Sportmax NSUs. John Surtees, who was now riding for MV, had a 'works' twin cam 203, Cecil Sandford had a 'works' Mondial, and ex-Brooklands rider Ron Harris of MV Concessionaires had begun to import the 125 and 175cc production racing MVs. In the face of this growing opposition, the British Special-builders appear to have remained undaunted.

1957 Clark 17th

Potts Norton

One of the new machines to appear in 1956 was the 250 Norton built by Joe Potts and ridden by Bob McIntyre. This was rumoured to be based on yet another ex-works Norton 350cc double overhead cam, outside flywheel engine. Rather than retain the original stroke of 72mm, as on the Frank Cope machine, Potts produced a one piece crankshaft with an ultra short stroke of 64mm. It had a plain bearing big end, and an alloy con rod with a split big end eye ran on shell-type bearings. In order to accommodate the short stroke, the mouth of the crankcases had to be machined down, and the cylinder barrel had only three fins. Access to the gudgeon pin proved to be extremely difficult during assembly. To overcome this, a hole was machined in the left hand crankcase, which was later sealed off by a flanged plate. The outside flywheel was retained and, with a cylinder bore of 71.5mm, the over-square engine could be run safely up to 8000rpm. The frame was a specially-built, lightweight duplex cradle 'featherbed' type, with Earles-type pivoted fork front suspension, and the wheels and brakes were also Manx Norton. During 1956, Bob McIntyre took the Potts Norton to a string of fourteen wins on British short circuits, including the 250cc British Championships at Thruxton.

Percy Tait continued to uphold Velocette honours with his Beasley, on which he had two wins at Cadwell Park and one at Scarborough, together with several other top three places. Londoner Roy Mayhew also began to make his mark on a 250 Velocette, allegedly one of the ex-Dearden works bikes, with wins at Brands Hatch and Silverstone as well as top places at most circuits. In fact, a feature of many 250 races in 1956 was a three-way battle between Percy Tait, Roy Mayhew and Dick Harding on the GMV, for the honour of being the highest placed British machine.

The steady influx of Continental machines continued in 1957. This was reflected in the entries for the 1957 Hutchinson 100, where only 26 of the 50 machines entered were of British origin, and of these 16 were either Manx Norton or KTT Velocette hybrids, with the latter proving to be more popular. This was in marked contrast to 1953, when British machines had made up 90% of the entry. However, the NSU Sportmax was still the only available production 250cc racing machine. Ron Harris also fielded a couple of a very fast ex-works, double overhead cam 125cc MVs, bored out to 203cc, which were virtually unbeatable in the hands of riders such as Mike O'Rourke and Dave Chadwick. Consequently, the British-built Specials were starting to be outclassed, but still continued to play an important supporting role in 250cc racing.

Bob McIntyre on the 250 Potts Norton, in the 1956 Hutchinson 100 at Silverstone.

Jimmy Buchan on the 250 Potts Norton, leading two Moto Guzzi riders and Percy Tait on a Beasley Velocette, at Scarborough in 1956.

Dan Shorey on the original version of the Beasley/Norvel, at Brands Hatch in 1957.

This picture of Dan Shorey on his Norvel, following John Dixon on an NSU Sportmax at Silverstone in April 1959, illustrates the struggle between the British-built Specials and the new Continental racing machines.

Dan Shorey at Scarborough in 1959. The Norvel now had a later-type Manx frame and twin leading shoe front brake.

Probably the only surviving 250 Petty Norton, belonging to Tony Horn from Berkshire.

Ivan Rhodes' ex-works 1951 Velo, with single overhead cam engine and four speed gearbox.

Close up of the 250 Petty Norton engine, with the unique stamping on the cam covers.

Norvel

Among the new Velocette exponents in 1957 were up-and-coming Dan Shorey from Banbury on his Norvel, and Jack Murgatroyd from Burnley on a Beasley Velocette. As the name suggests, the Shorey Norvel also used a Beasley engine and Velocette gearbox in a Norton 'featherbed' frame, with Norton forks, wheels and brakes. The Norvel engine used MOV flywheels, with KTT mainshafts and crankpin and a Mark 8 KTT con-rod, giving it a square bore and stroke of 68 x 68mm. The flywheels were stepped to allow piston clearance at the bottom of the stroke. When he bought the machine, it was fitted with a standard Mark 8 cam, but amongst the spares that came with it Dan Shorey found a Beasley camshaft, which he refitted and found an immediate increase in performance. By 1959, the Norvel had been updated with a later-type Manx frame and twin leading shoe front brake. Inevitably, however, it became less competitive against the new Continental machines and, in 1960, Dan acquired an NSU Sportmax.

The ex-Dave Chadwick/Reg Dearden RDS Velocette also reappeared briefly in 1957, ridden by Manxman George Costain who finished second in the Southern 100 (the race was won by Chester motorcycle dealer Bill Smith on yet another Beasley Velocette). Dick Harding, making a comeback after a bad crash on a 350 Norton at Mallory Park, had acquired the Benny Rood Velocette and had a win at Brands Hatch in July, and was second to Surtees' NSU at Crystal Palace in August. Unfortunately, the Rood Velocette hasn't survived intact, though the complete engine and gearbox assembly mounted on its engine plates still exists, and is presently owned by ex-racing man John Pinckney in Essex.

The Potts 250 Norton made only a few brief appearances in 1957, mainly at Errol and Crimmond, due to Bob McIntyre being on Grand Prix duty with the Gilera team. Ian Telfer entrusted his IFT to the very capable John Clark, a draughtsman from Portsmouth, who finished second to Mike O'Rourke's 203 MV at Castle Coombe in April. John also rode the IFT in the Lightweight TT, but was unfortunately suffering the after effects of a crash in the North West 200, and could only finish sixteenth.

Ian Telfer had also started to build a new machine, based on a Mark 8 KTT Velocette, which had over-square dimensions, a one piece crankshaft and an outside flywheel. He also built a new featherbed-type frame for it, using smaller diameter T45 tubing. The front forks were cut down Norton units, but the gearbox, wheels and brakes were Velocette KTT. The ITV (Ian Telfer Velocette), was raced briefly during 1958 and 1959 before being sold to Scottish rider Denis Gallagher, who had some success with it on Scottish circuits during the early 1960s.

Despite the presence of several more NSUs in 1958, Dan Shorey had wins at Cadwell Park, Rhydymwyn, and Silverstone Trophy Day on the Norvel, and was a consistent finisher in the top three at most National meetings. His main British-mounted rival, Jack Murgatroyd, continued to build up an impressive list of wins on his Beasley Velocette, mainly at northern circuits, such as Errol and Charterhall. The two riders finished third and fourth, respectively, in the ACU Road Racing Star competition in 1958. Percy Tait was also still in contention with his Beasley, taking a win at Thruxton on Easter Monday, and scoring several second and third places at his home circuit of Mallory Park.

Although the new Continental machines had become increasingly popular,

Norton and Velocette Specials continued to be raced well into the 1960s, even achieving some success, usually at some of the less important National meetings. Bob Rowe recorded some top three places with his 250 Norton in 1960/1961 at Crystal Palace and Brands Hatch. As previously mentioned, John Bacon raced a Petty Norton in 1960, as did John Williams, who was particularly successful at Prees Heath in 1961/1962. Another 250 Norton was raced by Barry Randall in 1963.

Most of the 250 Velocettes seemed to have found their way to Scotland, where they continued to do well on the northern and Scottish circuits, in the hands of riders like Bill Crosier and Dennis Gallagher.

Harry Whitehouse's fully restored Cope Norton, with modified Reynolds frame and front forks.

Evidence that some Beasley Velos are still in use today. This version, ridden by Jack Gooch, was seen at a recent CRMC meeting.

A close up showing engine details of the Jack Gooch Beasley Velocette.

Another example of an active Beasley Norvel, seen at the Nurburgring in 1994.

All that remains of Benny Rood's Velo: the engine and gearbox unit, showing the modified cam box and hairpin valve springs.

The NSU Sportmax which became available in 1955, and sounded the death knell for the British machines.

Chapter 4
BSA Gold Star Specials

During his five year sojourn at BSA, Roland Pike produced several 'test bed' 500cc Pike BSA Specials, based on both the single cylinder Gold Star and the twin cylinder BSA power units. Frustrated by the blinkered outlook that was prevalent in the boardrooms of the British motorcycle industry, Roland eventually left BSA, but in so doing he bequeathed a legacy of many experimental parts, and a great deal of technical data, which were later to form the basis for several BSA Gold Star-based 250cc machines.

GMS (Geoff Monty Special)

Probably the best known and most successful of the BSA Gold Star Specials was Geoff Monty's GMS, which appeared in 1956. Geoff had acquired Roland Pike's experimental 250cc Gold Star engine, which had a 61mm short stroke, one piece crankshaft and outside flywheel (the bore size remained standard at 72mm). A major contributory factor in the machine's performance was the modified cylinder head, in which the offset-angled inlet port had been blanked off and remachined centrally to provide a straight inlet tract with a steep downdraught angle. The engine produced just under 30bhp at 9400rpm, and was mounted in a lightweight, open spine frame designed by Geoff Monty. A large diameter top tube carried the steering head, and the engine was suspended from it where it curved down at the rear. The rear subframe consisted of a pair of large, $^5/_{16}$ inch (approx. 8.0mm), Dural plates, which supported the rear of the engine and the upright Manx Norton gearbox. The plates then continued upwards to join the main spine tube, and formed the side plates for the swinging arm pivot and the rear damper mountings. The swinging arm was of welded-up box section construction. From the steering head, two straight front down tubes terminated abruptly at crankcase level, and carried the plates that supported the

Mike O'Rourke enjoying a one-off ride on Geoff Monty's GMS in the 1958 Lightweight TT.

11ᵗʰ 68.57
Clypse Course

Tommy Robb, who was very successful with the GMS, is seen here in the 1959 Hutchinson 100 at Silverstone. He finished second, splitting the Mondials of Mike Hailwood and Jim Adam.

The GMS, which Dick Harding borrowed for a win at Brands Hatch in September 1957, when he beat Mike Hailwood on a 175 MV.

This picture of the GMS shows the frame construction, with the massive plates supporting the rear of the engine and the Norton upright gearbox. The large diameter spine tube can be seen between the seat nose and the carburettor bell mouth.

1959 Lightweight
1st 3 Provini, MV
Ubbiali, MV
Chadwick MV
4th Tommy Robb GMS
5th-9th All NSUs
Robb was also 4th in the Ulster

NB. Geoff Monty was 3rd
4th on the GMS in the
1958 Swedish GP at
Hedemora.

front of the engine. A feature of the design was the ability to remove the engine and gearbox from the frame as one complete unit. Shortened Manx Norton front forks were used, with Manx hubs and brakes front and rear in 18 inch wheels, and the complete bike weighed 254lb (approx. 115kg).

In his first major race on the GMS, at the Silverstone 'Saturday' meeting in April, Geoff finished fourth. The first win for the GMS was at Mallory Park on 3rd June and, during the 1956 season, Geoff had several well-deserved second places at Aintree, Blandford, Cadwell Park, Snetterton, Crystal Palace, the British Championships at Thruxton in August, and another win at Aintree in July. Roland Pike came out of retirement briefly in 1956 for a guest appearance on the GMS, and had a fourth place at the Silverstone 'Trophy Day' meeting on 7th July. It was a similar story during 1957 and 1958 when, in a limited racing programme, Geoff recorded a couple of wins at Snetterton, and several second places at Thruxton, Crystal Palace and Brands Hatch, often against foreign machinery which included John Surtees' NSU and MV, Cecil Sandford's Mondial, and Mike Hailwood's MV and NSU.

Geoff Monty retired from racing early in the 1959 season, and handed the GMS over to Tommy Robb who, during the next three years, became its most successful rider. He was particularly successful in Ireland, winning the 250cc North West 200 three years running, and scored class wins in the Mid-Antrim 100 and Temple 100. His fourth place in the 1959 Lightweight TT proved to be the best Isle of Man result for the GMS. On British short circuits he had wins at Blandford in May 1959, Snetterton in April 1960, and Brands Hatch in May 1960. He also achieved several rostrum places, which included a hard fought second place in the 1959 Hutchinson 100, when he split the Ecurie Sport Mondials of Mike Hailwood and Jim Adam. While Tommy was temporarily *'hors de combat'* following his TT practice crash in 1960, Alan Shepherd took over the GMS, achieving some commendable second places to Mike Hailwood, including a second place in the British Championships at Oulton Park. Geoff Monty's other sponsored rider, Ron Langston, also borrowed the GMS for a win at the Brands Hatch Yuletide meeting in December.

Tommy Robb recorded a last win for the GMS at Brands Hatch in May 1961, and also achieved some noteworthy second places to Mike Hailwood on Mondials and Honda fours. Although a second GMS was built for 1959, neither of the machines has survived. By 1963, the GMS was becoming uncompetitive, and after a few brief outings ridden by Monty & Ward employees Derek Warren and Dave Degens, both machines were broken up and Triumph 500 and 650cc engines were slotted into the frames to form the Triumph Monard Specials.

TTS (Tom Thorp Special)

The first BSA Gold Star-based 250 was probably the Special built by Dick Smith, who initially raced this machine in 1954. It was later raced by Tom Thorp, a pattern maker from Ruislip in Middlesex. The engine was based on a Roland Pike short stroke crankshaft assembly, but in all other respects the machine was basically a 350 Gold Star. Tom Thorp takes up the story: "Dick Smith asked me to ride the bike for him a couple of times, and in 1955 I had a win and second and third places on it at Brands Hatch. I eventually bought the bike from him and began to develop it myself, calling it the TTS".

Over the next few years, Tom Thorp further modified the TTS. The BSA Gold Star frame was discarded in favour of a specially-built lightweight frame, and the BSA gearbox was changed for an Albion five speed racing unit. One of the reasons for the change to the Albion gearbox, was due to the bottom gear on the BSA close-ratio cluster being too high for a 250cc machine. The crankshaft was changed for a new one-piece assembly with an external flywheel and a split connecting rod running in plain bearings. The cylinder head was also modified along the lines of the GMS, in which the inlet port was welded up and re-machined along the central axis of the cylinder head. This helped to push the maximum revs up to 9000rpm. Between 1957 and 1959, the TTS was one of the more successful British machines at National level, and Tom Thorp achieved a couple of wins and several second and third places, particularly at Brands Hatch. The final version of the TTS had a spine-type frame with a large diameter front down tube which carried five pints (2.8 litres) of engine oil. It was ridden by Tom Thorp until the early 1960s, when it continued to do well among the British machines, and was second to the GMS in the 1960 North West 200. Ian Goddard rode the TTS during its final racing period, around 1962.

Pike BSA

Another rider to follow the Pike school, was Gerry Turner of Rudge fame, who had taken over the 350 and 500 Pike BSAs following Denis Lashmar's fatal accident in 1954. Using the drawings supplied by Roland Pike, Gerry built another 250 Pike BSA around 1957/1958. The crankshaft was turned out by fellow racer Tom Thorp from nearby Ruislip, and the engine, which had a bore and stroke of 71 x 63mm, and the BSA gearbox were mounted in a Pike-type frame. An unusual feature of the machine was the Rudge front brake, modified to two leading shoe operation by Gerry Turner, who preferred it to the standard Gold Star brake. The BSA made its TT debut in 1958, when it finished fifteenth in the Lightweight TT on the Clypse circuit. However, before the machine's full potential could be developed, Gerry was involved in a bad crash in 1959, in which he was hit by a following rider, and suffered severe head injuries which ended his racing career.

Hoff BSA

Another 250 BSA Gold Star was built in 1955 by Sydney Hoff, who was the manager of a motorcycle dealership in Leicester. Several versions of this machine were built using different engines. The first engine retained the 71mm bore, but the crankshaft was modified to provide a 63mm stroke. This required a shortened cylinder barrel and a specially-manufactured, shorter connecting rod. Two other versions were built, one with square dimensions of 68 x 68mm using a modified flywheel assembly with an offset crankpin, and a third version, which reverted to the 71 x 63mm dimensions. All three versions used a standard BSA flywheel assembly. The engines were mounted in a BSA Gold Star frame with a modified large diameter top tube, BSA wheels and forks. The BSA gearbox was replaced by an upright Manx Norton unit. The early versions of this bike were raced by Coventry rider John Eckart in 1956, at Mallory Park and Alton Towers.

In 1958, a radical change was made to the crankshaft assembly along the lines of the Roland Pike engines. A one-piece crankshaft was turned from a sold billet, and the connecting rod ran on plain bearings. An outside flywheel was splined onto the drive side mainshaft. The engine dimensions remained at 71 x 63mm. Over the next couple of years, the Hoff BSA was ridden by Nottingham rider Freddie Wallis who demonstrated the machine's potential in 1959 with wins at Mallory Park and Cadwell Park in March, and another win at Cadwell in August, as well as second and third places at Aberdare Park.

Several other BSA Gold Star-based 250s were built and raced into the early 1960s with a modicum of success, until the arrival of new factory-produced racing machines. Some of these machines, such as the Blackwell Special, the Jones Edwards Special, and a replica of the GMS, still exist today, carefully looked after by their enthusiastic owners, and even appearing occasionally at Historic events.

A very early version of the TTS, circa 1955, which had a modified crankshaft and cylinder barrel to reduce the capacity to 250cc, but was still basically a BSA Gold Star. (Courtesy Tom Thorp)

Gerry Turner on his 250 Pike BSA at Edges Corner on the Clypse circuit, in the 1958 Lightweight TT.

Tom Thorp on a much later version of the TTS. By now, the use of a fairing has obscured most of the technical details, but the large diameter front down tube which carried the engine oil can just be seen behind the front wheel. (Courtesy Tom Thorp)

Chapter 5
Other Specials

LEF

Although the post-war 350cc twin cylinder Triumph 3T was not a popular choice for racing, its engine was chosen as the basis for the LEF. This was built by Bob Foster and Herbert Lewis, partners in the motorcycle dealership of Lewis, Ellis and Foster (hence LEF), in Watford, Hertfordshire. This machine started life as a grass track machine, using the original Triumph engine. Around 1948, however, it was decided to convert the machine into a 250cc road racer. To reduce the capacity to 250cc, Foster and Lewis machined a completely new crankshaft, with a 52.5mm stroke, from solid billets (the original 55mm

The 1949 version of the LEF.

cylinders were retained). Tiger 100 alloy connecting rods were used to achieve the desired piston height. The standard 3T cylinder head was modified to accept two inlet stubs for the twin standard Amal carburettors. In this form, and with the original rigid frame, the machine was raced in 1948 by John Harrowell at Ansty near Coventry and Eppynt in mid-Wales.

For 1949, the frame was modified to swinging arm rear suspension, using Newton shock absorbers, and Herbert Lewis designed some new camshafts to produce a bit more power at the top end. John Harrowell had some promising results at Haddenham and Eppynt,

Left to right: John Harrowell, Bob Foster and Herbert Lewis, with the LEF at the Isle of Man in 1949.

John Harrowell on the LEF at Eppynt in 1949.

John Harrowell (LEF) at Haddenham in 1949. Following is Les Archer Jnr on an MOV Velo.

The 1950 LEF frame.

Bob Foster with his LEF in 1950.

Denis Lashmar, who took over riding duties on the LEF, at the one and only Goodwood meeting in April 1951.

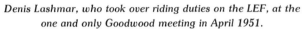

before going to the TT where, unfortunately, he was forced to retire on the last lap due to a broken primary chain. A completely new frame was built for 1950 using ex-WD oval section tubing. A new light alloy cylinder head with straight exhaust ports was designed and cast locally, and an Albion racing gearbox was fitted. The engine revved to 9000rpm giving it a top speed of around 90mph (145 km/h). With its slab-sided, moulded fuel tank, centrally-mounted wrap-round oil tank, alloy mudguards and wheel rims, flat racing seat, and megaphone exhaust system, the LEF had a purposeful look about it.

For 1951, a new cylinder head was produced from a higher grade of light alloy. Aluminium bronze skulls were cast in to form the combustion chambers. Inlet valve sizes were increased to 11/16 inch (approx. 27mm), and longer induction pipes were used. Unfortunately, John I-Iarrowell was forced to retire from racing due to work commitments, but not before he scored a second place at Eppynt on 5th May. Dennis Lashmar took over the LEF for the rest of the year, scoring a third at Boreham on 1st September. By 1952, Lewis and Foster decided that the pushrod twin had reached the end of its development, and decided to build a slave double overhead cam, single cylinder 125, with a view to scaling it up to a 250cc twin later. The superb, but extremely noisy little 125, was ridden by Jim Dakin and Eric Pantlin, and proved to be quite successful for a couple of years, despite opposition from several production racer MVS. Its most noteworthy performance was a fifth place in the 1956 TT, ridden by the talented Dave Chadwick.   60.25 Clypse

The 250 twin and the 125 have been restored to running condition and remain in the care of Bob Foster's son Rob. Both machines have appeared from time to time at Hiistoric events.

7R AJS

Strangely enough, the 7R AJS didn`t appear to be as popular a machine for conversion to 250cc as the Norton and Velocette. The best known example being the Frank Cope machine which appeared in 1948, the year in which the 7R was first introduced. It was ridden by Frank in the 1948 Manx Grand Prix, and then mostly in the TT until 1952 where it recorded two eighth places in 1950 and 1951. The technical details of this machine have been difficult to trace, and the evidence seems to suggest that its bore was sleeved down to reduce the capacity, but it was, in all other respects, a standard 7R AJS.

JEL (Jones, Earles, Lomas)

There certainly seemed to be no shortage of talented engineers during the 1950s. Dennis Jones from Long Eaton, for example, was another engineer in the same mould as Bob Geeson. Jones produced several racing engines over the years, ranging from a supercharged four cylinder two stroke, to a 500cc four cylinder four stroke. One of his projects was a twin cylinder, double overhead cam 250, with a bore and stroke of 54 x 54 mm. The camshafts were driven by a train of gears from the right hand end of the four bearing crankshaft, and the connecting rods ran on plain bearings.

In 1955, Bill Lomas borrowed this engine from Dennis Jones with the intention of developing it further. The big end bearings were changed to caged roller types and, with a new camshaft, higher compression pistons and 27mm carburettors, the power output was increased from 20.5bhp at 8500rpm to 28bhp at 10,000rpm. At first, the big end bearings couldn't withstand prolonged running at 10,000rpm without breaking up. This was eventually cured by

Frank Cope 7R AJS

T.T.   1950   8th   68.73
        1951   8th   70.00
        1952   15th   71.37
        1953   13th   70.23
ULSTER 1950   9th

increasing the side clearance on the connecting rods and the machine then performed quite well, with a top speed of 107mph (173km/h). The gearbox was a five speed Albion racing unit.

Ernie Earles was commissioned to build a new frame for the engine, and produced a full duplex cradle frame similar to the one used for the Lomas 125 MV in 1953. The original Earles forks were later changed for a pair of Velocette telescopics.

The bike was named the JEL (Jones, Earles, Lomas), and Bill Lomas entered himself on it for the Lightweight TT Fate intervened, however, when he was offered a works 203 MV at the last minute. Bill then went to live in Italy to ride for Moto Guzzi and never rode the JEL. The project was handed back to Dennis Jones and, over the next couple of years it was ridden occasionally by several riders, including Len King and Pete Tomes. Tomes demonstrated its potential by gaining second places at Thruxton and Cadwell Park.

Ronald Peck Special

Another name probably familiar to racing enthusiasts from the classic period is Ronald Peck, an engineering draughtsman from Redbourne in Hertfordshire. Like Denis Jones, Peck wasn't primarily motivated by road racing, and in fact both the JEL and the RPS (Ronald Peck Special), were initially conceived purely as engineering exercises.

Peck started work on his engine in the early 1950s. The design was for a unit construction, gear-driven double overhead cam, four cylinder 250, with engine dimensions of 44 x 41mm. The engine was finally completed in 1953 and, as an interim measure, it was mounted in a New Imperial frame with modified girder front forks and swinging arm rear suspension. Later, the RPS was given a new featherbed-type frame, with Earles-type front forks. Leighton Buzzard engineer Syd Mularney acquired the machine in 1958, and it finally made its first track appearance at the Silverstone 'Saturday' meeting in April, ridden by Brian Setchell. Over a period of several years, Syd Mularney spent a great deal of time trying to develop the machine, but without success, and around 1965 he finally gave up and sold the machine.

Phoenix JAP

As the name suggests, this was the rather unique combination of a speedway JAP engine in a special frame. It was built in 1952 by Ernie Barrett, an engineer from Tottenham in London, who had been racing in the TT and on short circuits (on Nortons, 7R AJS and a 250 Moto Guzzi), for several years. The JAP engine had an alloy head and barrel, but employed dry sump lubrication instead of the usual speedway total loss system. Both 250 and 350cc versions were built, and the engines and Norton gearbox were mounted in featherbed-type duplex cradle frames, with Earles-type, pivoted fork front suspension. The 250cc version was initially fairly successful in 1953, with a second place to Maurice Cannls Guzzi at Crystal Palace on June 28th, a win at Brands Hatch on July 19th, and a twelfth place in the Lightweight TT The 250 was raced fairly regularly until 1956/ 1957, scoring the occasional rostrum finish. At least one of the machines is believed to have survived complete and intact until quite recently.

1953 12th 71.09
1954 17th 64.22

EMC

The British Ehrlich Motor Company entered the fray once again in 1952, when

*Ernie Barret on his 250 Phoenix JAP,
followed by Brian Purslow on the Beasley/
Earles Velo at Scarborough in 1955.
(Courtesy VMCC Archives)*

*The JEL in 1955. The dolphin fairing
carried the side-mounted pannier tanks.*

Engine detail of the JEL, showing the mounting for the twin carbs, the massive casting housing the camshaft drive, and the specially-built Earles frame, with Velocette forks.

Ronald Peck with his 250 four cylinder Special in 1958.

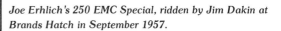

Joe Erhlich's 250 EMC Special, ridden by Jim Dakin at Brands Hatch in September 1957.

it marketed 125cc production racers, which proved to be quite popular and fairly successful for a while. Joe Ehrlich also built a special 250 which proved to be less successful, however, although Dudley Edlin had a win at Crystal Palace and scored some podium places on it in 1957. These EMCS, however, were an amalgamation of the Austrian Puch two stroke, split single engines, with British-built frames and components.

EMK

The EM Kempson Special was built for Teddy Kempson around 1956, by the ever-ingenious Ron Mead. The crankcases were designed and cast by Mead, and contained a special, short stroke crankshaft assembly with an outside flywheel. A KTT Velocette cylinder barrel and double overhead cam cylinder head were used. The camshafts were driven by a single enclosed chain from a sprocket driven from the right hand side of the crankshaft. The large triangular-shaped timing chain cover gave the engine a distinctive appearance. Twin plug coil ignition was used with a contact breaker mounted on the end of the inlet camshaft. The engine was slotted into a 'featherbed' Manx Norton rolling chassis which Teddy had acquired from Steve Lancefield, and a Manx Norton gearbox and clutch were used. The EMK was raced by Teddy Kempson from 1956 to 1958 and achieved a modicum of success, including a couple of third places at Brands Hatch. However, although the machine had potential, developing such a unique machine proved difficult without the assistance of Ron Mead, who moved back to the north of England shortly after the EMK was built.

The EMK at the Hutchinson 100 in 1956, with Teddy Kempson and his friend, and mechanic, Bob Tyler. (Courtesy Ted Kempson)

EMK engine details showing the camshaft drive, inlet camshaft-driven contact breaker, and twin plug head. (Courtesy Ted Kempson)

Drive side of the EMK showing the flywheel outside the engine sprocket. (Courtesy Ted Kempson)

Ted Kempson in action on the EMK at Brands Hatch in 1956. (Courtesy Ted Kempson)

Chapter 6
Epilogue

By 1959, construction of new British 250cc Specials had virtually come to an end. Since 1957, the 250cc class had been dominated by Mike Hailwood, first with his NSU Sportmax, and later Ducati and Mondial. Inevitably, several other riders, including Fron Purslow, Jack Murgatroyd and Dan Shorey, also acquired Sportmax NSUS in order to remain competitive. The NSU factory had also produced a race kit for the roadster Supermax, which converted it into quite a useful and popular machine. The growing popularity of Continental machines was reflected in the entries for the 1959 Hutchinson 100 when, out of a total of 50, 20 were NSUs. Various 175 and 203cc MVs had also filtered down to private hands, and there was the usual handful of Moto Guzzis. The superior performance of the purpose-built German and Italian machines had made many of the British Specials uncompetitive.

In September 1960, Alan Shepherd scored a debut win at Scarborough on the first of the new 250 Aermacchis A year or two later, Dan Shorey started racing a 196cc Bultaco, the success of which led to the introduction of a full 250cc version. British manufacturers finally woke up to the value of 250cc racing, and a minor renaissance took place in the British motorcycle industry. Greeves and Cotton almost simultaneously announced a new generation of 250cc production racers for 1963, soon to be followed by DMW and Royal Enfield. It was the availability of these new British and Continental factory-produced racing machines that led to the demise of the basically home-built British Specials. Those unique machines, however, epitomise an era during which the engineering skills and ingenuity of private individuals formed the backbone of racing, and kept the 250cc class in Britain alive for more than a decade.

Index